West's Law School
Advisory Board

JESSE H. CHOPER
Professor of Law,
University of California, Berkeley

JOSHUA DRESSLER
Professor of Law, Michael E. Moritz College of Law,
The Ohio State University

YALE KAMISAR
Professor of Law, University of San Diego
Professor of Law, University of Michigan

MARY KAY KANE
Professor of Law, Chancellor and Dean Emeritus,
University of California,
Hastings College of the Law

LARRY D. KRAMER
Dean and Professor of Law, Stanford Law School

JONATHAN R. MACEY
Professor of Law, Yale Law School

ARTHUR R. MILLER
University Professor, New York University
Professor of Law Emeritus, Harvard University

GRANT S. NELSON
Professor of Law, Pepperdine University
Professor of Law Emeritus, University of California, Los Angeles

A. BENJAMIN SPENCER
Associate Professor of Law,
Washington & Lee University School of Law

JAMES J. WHITE
Professor of Law, University of Michigan

REPRESENTING THE PROFESSIONAL ATHLETE

By

Peter A. Carfagna

Visiting Lecturer in Sports Law
Harvard Law School
Senior Counsel
Calfee, Halter & Griswold, LLP

AMERICAN CASEBOOK SERIES®

A Thomson Reuters business

Mat #40805598

American Casebook Series is a trademark registered in the U.S. Patent and Trademark Office.

© 2009 Thomson Reuters
    610 Opperman Drive
    St. Paul, MN 55123
    1–800–313–9378

Printed in the United States of America

ISBN: 978–0–314–20441–7

TEXT IS PRINTED ON 10% POST
CONSUMER RECYCLED PAPER

Acknowledgment

I would like to thank all of the people at Thomson Reuters and at Harvard Law School who so ably assisted me in preparing and editing this book. In particular, I would like to thank then-Dean Elena Kagan (now Solicitor General of the United States) for giving me the opportunity to serve as the Covington and Burling Distinguished Visitor at my alma mater. I would also like to thank my good friend Professor Paul Weiler for his Sports Law scholarship and guidance since he first taught me and supervised my third-year paper at Harvard in 1979. Paul continues to serve as an inspiration for me and for all of us who teach or practice sports law today. It is truly a singular privilege for me to be able to offer this book as a "companion" to Paul's "magnum opus," *Sports and the Law*, without reference to which no legal education in this field could be complete.

I would also like to thank Lande Spottswood, my teaching assistant at Harvard Law School during spring semester 2008, who took the lead in transforming my Harvard Law School course into the current text. Lande's many contributions, along with those of her '08 Harvard Law School classmates, Paul Breaux, Ben Huston and Mike Menitove, made the publication of this book possible. I sincerely want to thank these students for their efforts, and wish them the best of luck in pursuing their "dream," which I have been fortunate enough to realize, of "representing the professional athlete!"

Finally, I would like to thank my wife Rita, my sisters Rosemarie and Jeanne, and the rest of my family for supporting me throughout my tenure as a Visiting Lecturer in Sports Law at Harvard Law School. Without their support and encouragement, the completion of this project would not have been possible.

*

Summary of Contents

Table of Contents

*

Table of Cases

References are to Pages

*

REPRESENTING THE PROFESSIONAL ATHLETE

*

Chapter 1

THE LEGAL RELATIONSHIP BETWEEN THE ATHLETE- AGENT AND THE CLIENT[1]

The relationship between an agent and his client is governed by various state statutes and league regulations, as well as two separate but interrelated bodies of law: (1) the law of agency; and (2) contract law. Once an athlete-agent relationship has been established, an agent is considered a fiduciary of the athlete under the law of agency. The agent then has a set of legal obligations, called "fiduciary duties," which compel him to put the interests of the athlete ahead of his own interests during business dealings. Against this general backdrop of agency law, which applies to all agent-athlete relationships, the athlete and agent also operate under a contract, which is specific to their relationship. The contract may be based on an oral agreement or "handshake" deal, or it may be memorialized in a written document, called the representation agreement.

This chapter begins with an introduction to the fiduciary duties that apply to all agents in Section A. Section B then examines some particularly egregious examples of agents who breached their fiduciary duties and the resulting efforts of legislative bodies, the NCAA and players associations to address agent misconduct. Finally, Section C turns towards the contractual relationship between the athlete and the agent with a detailed examination of the representation agreement, from the point of view of the drafter.

---

1. For further background on the case law pertaining to the fiduciary and contractual duties of agents, see the companion book, Weiler, Sports and the Law, 383–430.

A. An Introduction to Agency Law & Fiduciary Duty

The agent, as a fiduciary of the athlete, must act on behalf of the athlete "with respect to matters within the scope of his agency."[2] While the law may vary slightly from state to state, a breach of fiduciary duty typically has three elements: (1) the existence of a duty arising from a fiduciary relationship; (2) a failure to observe the duty; and (3) an injury resulting proximately from the breach.[3] Because of the breadth of the test, allegations that an agent has breached his fiduciary duties may come in a wide variety of contexts.

The most common allegations of a breach of fiduciary duty involve three situations: (1) when an agent acts in a way that increases the compensation the agent receives, perhaps at the expense of the athlete; (2) when the agent has a conflict of interest, such as another client competing for the same endorsement deal, that may incentivize the agent to consider another party's interests other than the athlete's; and (3) when the agent acts negligently or negligently fails to act on the client's behalf. These three common scenarios do not cover, however, the most flagrant breaches of fiduciary duty, such as when an agent steals from his client. This blatant agent misconduct, which potentially creates both criminal and civil liability, will be discussed in Section B.

The first major allegation of an agent breaching his fiduciary duty to his client in order to maximize his own compensation came against one of the first major sports agents—the late Bob Woolf. One of Woolf's NHL clients, Andrew Brown, was weighing competing offers from his current team, the Pittsburgh Penguins, and the Indianapolis Pacers of the upstart World Hockey League. The Penguins offered Brown a two-year contract, worth $80,000 each year, though the contract was not guaranteed. The Pacers countered with a five-year, guaranteed contract at $160,000 per season. Woolf advised Brown to accept the Pacers offer—perhaps because Woolf was entitled to a five percent commission on any contract— and Brown followed his advice. Soon after Brown signed on with the Pacers, however, the team encountered financial problems, which eventually led to bankruptcy. In pre-bankruptcy negotiations with the financially-strapped squad, Woolf secured only $185,000 of the $800,000 guaranteed to Brown, while managing to recover his full $40,000 commission on the contract from the Pacers. When Brown discovered the payment, he sued Woolf on grounds of breach of fiduciary duty and material misrepresentation. In *Brown v.*

---

2. § 13, Restatement (2d) of Agency.
3. These are the elements in Ohio, for example, as stated in *Heights Driv-* *ing Sch. v. Motorists Ins. Co.,* 2003 Ohio 1737 (Ct. App. 2003).

Woolf,[4] the court refused to grant summary judgment, finding instead that there was a "question of fact" as to whether or not there was constructive fraud due to "the making of a false statement, by the dominant party in a ... fiduciary relationship ... upon which the plaintiff reasonably relied to his detriment." While the case was never resolved on the merits, the legal standard cited by the judge helps illuminate the higher standard to which fiduciaries are held.

Another example of a conflict between the athlete and the agent's financial interest came in *Jones v. Childers*[5] and *Hernandez v. Childers.*[6] In those cases, Gordon Jones (of the Tampa Bay Buccaneers) and Keith Hernandez (of the New York Mets) alleged that their agent John Childers breached his fiduciary duties when he counseled them to invest in high-risk, non-IRS approved tax shelters. While the clients ended up losing money on the investments, Childers received a commission from the company that he failed to disclose the commission to his clients. In both cases, the courts found a breach of fiduciary duty.

The second common type of case brought against agents for breach of fiduciary duty allege that an agent failed to properly disclose a conflict of interest or allowed a conflict of interest to interfere with his fiduciary duties. One particularly flagrant example is explained in the case of *Detroit Lions & Billy Sims v. Jerry Argovitz.*[7] Billy Sims was a star running back for the Detroit Lions. His agent, Jerry Argovitz, had recently become a part owner of the Houston Gamblers of the USFL. When Sims' contract expired, Argovitz—without notifying Sims as to the extent of his interest in the Gamblers—represented Sims in negotiations with both the Lions and the Gamblers. When the Lions refused to offer Sims a guaranteed contract, negotiations broke down. Sims "believed that the organization was not that interested in him and his pride was wounded." The next week, Argovitz and Sims entered into face-to-face negotiations with the Gamblers, who topped the Lions' financial offer and also guaranteed the contract. Sims wanted to sign right away, but Argovitz told his client that the Lions would likely match the Gamblers financial package. Argovitz asked Sims if he should call the Lions for a final offer, and the client declined. Sims then agreed to the deal with the Gamblers. At that moment, the court found:

"Argovitz irreparably breached his fiduciary duty. As agent for Sims, he had the duty to telephone the Lions, receive its final offer, and present the terms of both offers to Sims. Only then could it be

4. 554 F. Supp. 1206 (S.D. Ind. 1983).

5. 18 F.3d 899 (11th Cir. 1994).

6. 806 F.Supp. 1368 (N.D. Ill. 1992).

7. 580 F.Supp. 542 (E. D. Mich. 1984)

said that Sims made an intelligent and knowing decision to accept the Gamblers Offer. . . . Although it is generally true that an agent is not liable for losses occurring as a result of following his principal's instructions, this rule of law is not applicable when the agent has placed himself in a position adverse to that of his principal."

The court declared Sims' contract with the Gamblers unenforceable. It also refused to enforce a waiver signed by Sims at the time of the contract, which waived any claims against Argovitz, because Sims did not have independent legal counsel.

It is worth noting, however, that Argovitz went on to prevail in another case alleging conflict of interest. In that case, Argovitz represented Gary Anderson, whom he allegedly "channeled" to the USFL's Tampa Bay Bandits instead of to an NFL franchise, because of his interests in the USFL. When Anderson later tried to back out of the contract, a Texas judge enjoined him from playing in the NFL, upholding the contract between Anderson and the Bandits despite Argovitz's failure to disclose his financial interests in the USFL.

The conflicts of interest faced by sports agents continue to grow as the industry becomes more consolidated, with agencies often comprising just one part of a media conglomerate. In August of 2000, for example, Clear Channel Communications acquired SFX—the home of super agents David Falk and Arn Tellem,[8] among others—for $4.4 billion, creating an immediate conflict of interest. The problem? Clear Channel's vice chairman Tom Hicks owned both the Dallas Stars of the NHL and the Texas Rangers of the MLB. One of Clear Channel's major shareholders, Red McCombs, owned the Minnesota Vikings of the NFL. These unavoidable conflicts of interest necessitated a corporate restructuring, with an autonomous division for negotiating player contracts. Other conflicts of interest arise when individual agents, like Argovitz, invest in teams or leagues. In 2007, for example, veteran NFL executive and player agent Michael Hyughue, whose client list included Adam "Pac Man" Jones, voluntarily relinquished his certification to represent NFL players when he accepted a position as the Commissioner of the upstart United Football League.

The third and final common type of claim athletes bring against their agents alleges breach of fiduciary duty for negligently failing to perform the duties owed to the athlete. These suits often also involve breach of contract claims, alleging that the agent did not carry out his obligations under the representation agreement.

8. At the time, Falk represented Michael Jordan and Tellem represented Kobe Bryant, among others.

One particularly tragic example was the case of Len Bias, the No. 2 pick in the 1986 NBA draft. When Bias died from an overdose of cocaine two days after the draft, his family brought suit against his agent Lee Fentress, alleging that he negligently failed to finalize agreements before Bias' death. The court, however, found that the agent did not act negligently and that a reasonable person would not expect Fentress to finalize the contracts within two days of the draft.[9]

B. Agent Misconduct & Fund Mismanagement

As discussed in the previous section, the interests of agents and athletes can oftentimes be at odds, creating incentives for agents to breach their fiduciary duties. Typically, this only results in civil or contractual liability or an equitable remedy, such as nullification of a contract. In some cases, however, an agent's actions may be so flagrant that they result in criminal liability. Such actions are the subject of this section.

Most potentially criminal conduct by agents involves the mismanagement of their clients' funds. Because some athletes are not sophisticated in financial matters, they rely heavily upon their agents to manage their funds. Such reliance has cost many athletes large portions of their fortunes, as agents have invested in extremely risky ventures and even flat out stolen funds.

The first, and most famous example, was Don King's representation of Mike Tyson, the former heavyweight champion. From the outset of King and Tyson's long-term relationship, Tyson relied heavily on King. After only three months of representation, Tyson granted King power of attorney privileges over his finances. "I authorized him to look out for me and my money and to make sure we don't have any tax problems," Tyson said. "I would do anything he told me to do." In 1998, with his finances in ruin despite having earned some $300 million in purses during his career, Tyson commenced litigation against King, alleging breach of contract and fiduciary duty, seeking to recover $100 million in damages. King, according to several of his former employees, had billed Tyson for various personal and unauthorized expenses throughout the representation, including company holiday bonuses, limousine charges, political donations, traveling expenses and a Manhattan condominium. King countersued for $110 million, but after years of litigation and discovery, eventually settled the claims in 2004 by promising to pay Tyson $14 million. Tyson, who was by then in bankruptcy with $38 million in debt, never received the money, which went directly to his creditors.

9. *Bias v. Advantage International, Inc.*, 905 F.2d 1558 (D.C. Cir. 1990).

While King has (thus far) managed to skirt criminal prosecution in relation to his management of client funds,[10] other agents have not been as lucky. The most infamous recent example is William "Tank" Black. Black—the head of the South Carolina-based agency, Professional Management, Inc.—represented mostly NFL players, along with NBA all-star Vince Carter. Black convinced two of his NFL clients, Fred Taylor and Ike Hilliard, to invest millions in two fraudulent investment schemes: (1) Black Americans of Achievement, Inc. (of which Black was the president), which was producing a board game on the achievements of African-Americans; and (2) Cash 4 Titles, a company offering high-interest car loans to customers with bad credit. The money earmarked for those investments actually went to Black's personal account in the Cayman Islands. When Taylor and Hilliard discovered the fraud, they filed suit against Black alleging breach of fiduciary duty and fraud. The players won, but were not able to recoup their losses, because at that time Black was judgment proof. Black was not saved from criminal liability, however. In 2001, a federal judge sentenced Black to six years in prison on federal charges of money laundering. The next Spring, Black was also sentenced to an additional five years in prison for defrauding Taylor and Hilliard, along with other clients.

In a strange legal twist, however, Black prevailed in separate litigation brought by Vince Carter, arguing that Black's breach of fiduciary duty was grounds to retroactively terminate their 12–year representation agreement without penalty. The agreement, which was signed in 1999, required that either party pay the other $3 million to terminate the agreement before the term expired. When Black was first accused of swindling his NFL clients in 2000, Carter split up with Black and signed with International Management Group (IMG). After Black was convicted of money laundering and fraud, he came after Carter for breach of contract, suing him for $9 million in back-due commissions on endorsement deals Black had secured for Carter as well as $5 million in contractual damages. Carter countersued for monies lost in a shoe deal that fell apart during Black's legal troubles, as well as the $3 million termination fee and monies lost due to Black's fraudulent mismanagement of Carter's funds. The federal court in South Carolina, however, relied on the language of the representation agreement to find in favor of Black, ordering Carter to pay Black $4.7 million in commissions owed under the contract. This finding was in spite of the fact that

---

10. In 1984, King was convicted of second-degree murder for beating to death a man who owed him money. The judge reduced the sentence to manslaughter, and King served a three-and-a-half year sentence before being pardoned by Ohio governor James Rhodes. While he was later investigated for tax fraud, racketeering and conspiracy, King was never convicted.

the same jury also held that Black violated his fiduciary duties, and had to refund some $800,000 in monies borrowed from Carter.

King and Carter are only the most famous in a long line of agents who have taken financial advantage of their clients. In 1998, John Gillette of Pro Sports Management pled guilty to 37 counts of grand theft and one of forgery after swindling clients, including Darren Woodson, Junior Seau and Eric Chavez, out of more than $11 million in investments. Gillette was sentenced to 10 years in state prison. In the same year, Canadian Alan Eagleson, a former executive director of the NHLPA with some 150 NHL clients also was convicted on federal charges. After being caught skimming money from players' pension funds and disability payments, Eagleson pled guilty to three counts of mail fraud and three counts of fraud in Toronto, before serving six months in a Canadian prison.

Similarly, Richard Sorkin had his clients sign representation agreements providing that all of their endorsement earnings be sent directly to him. After losing almost $1 million of client funds through the stock market and gambling debts, Sorkin pled guilty to seven counts of grand larceny.

C. *The Regulation of Athlete Agents*

In response to the misconduct of agents, various bodies have implemented agent regulations. State legislatures, the NCAA, and the various players associations are among those groups that currently police the actions of agents. This section will focus mainly on the state legislatures and the players associations. The NCAA rules governing agents, and how their actions may affect amateur eligibility, are addressed in Chapter 2, on Recruiting Clients.

California enacted the first state law regulating agents in 1982 as the "Athletic Agents Act." The Athletic Agents Act broadly protected all athletes from various agent abuses, but subsequent state legislation focused far more on agents' interactions with collegiate athletes. The Uniform Athlete Agent Act (UAAA), which was drafted by the National Conference of Commissioners on Uniform State Laws in 2000, focuses on the harm done to amateur athletes and their universities when athletes sign with agents before their eligibility has expired. Along with requiring registration, the UAAA also regulates the interactions of the agent with amateur athletes in several ways, including:

(1) requiring that all representation agreements be in writing, signed by both parties, and contain clear provisions specifying agent compensation;

(2) prohibiting agents from offering "anything of value to any person to induce a student athlete" to enter into a representation agreement;

(3) requiring that each representation agreement contain a bold legend warning the student-athlete that signing the contract will make him ineligible for intercollegiate competition; and

(4) compelling the agent to notify the athlete's school that a representation agreement has been signed within 72 hours or before the next game in which the athlete will compete.

The UAAA also gives student-athletes a 14–day grace period to change their mind and nullify a contract and creates a cause of action for any university damaged by the agent's failure to notify it of an athlete's ineligibility, allowing recovery for damages incurred due to NCAA sanctions. Unlike the Athletic Agents Act, the UAAA—which has been adopted by 36 states and Washington D.C. through 2007—arguably protects collegiate athletics and not individual athletes.

The players associations' regulations of agents, meanwhile, focus more on potential harm to individual athletes. The NFLPA first adopted a set of regulations for "contract advisors" in 1983, and with several variations, the NBPA (1985), the MLBPA (1987), and the NHLPA (1995) followed its lead in subsequent years. The unions' authority to impose regulations on agents comes from labor law, which provides that a union has exclusive authority to represent all of its members for purposes of collective bargaining. When it comes to individual bargaining over player salaries, the unions conditionally delegate their authority to represent the athletes to agents of which they approve, and *only* to agents of which they approve. This practice has withstood antitrust scrutiny, on the grounds that the regulation of agents falls under the non-statutory labor exemption.[11] On this theory, the various unions compel registration of agents, impose restrictions on agent compensation (particularly on compensation for negotiating playing contracts), require agents to disclose certain conflicts of interest and prohibit other types of conflicts of interest, and restrict what agents can offer prospective clients to induce them to sign a representation agreement. For example, the NFLPA prohibits agents from: (1) receiving any payments from teams; (2) "[p]roviding or offering money or any other thing of value to any player or prospective player to induce or encourage that player to utilize his/her services" or to the player's family members; (3) failing to "disclose in writing to any player ... any fee paid or received by Contract Advisor to or

---

11. *Collins v. NBPA & Grantham,* 976 F.2d 740 (10th Cir. 1992). For more on the non-statutory labor exemption, see Chapter 3 "From Antitrust to Labor Law" in Sports and the Law.

from a third party in return for providing services to that player."[12] The NFLPA, and other unions, have separate rules and regulations governing financial advisers.

Two interesting legal issues surround the unions' regulation of agents. First, how much discretion do the unions have in choosing whom to certify an agent? And second, if the unions certify agents that later defraud athletes, can the unions be held accountable for negligence? The first question was addressed in an arbitration involving Barry Rona. The MLBPA had rejected Rona's application to be an agent under a regulation barring anyone whose conduct "may adversely affect his credibility or integrity . . . . to serve in a representative and/or fiduciary capacity on behalf of players." The MLBPA reasoned that, because Rona had served as General Counsel and as an Executive Director of MLB during a time period when the owners illegally colluded to depress players salaries, Rona could not be trusted to act as a fiduciary to the players he sought to represent. NYU law professor Daniel Collins, sitting as an arbitrator, held that the MLBPA's refusal to certify Rona was "arbitrary and capricious" and therefore could be overturned.

After several particularly flagrant cases of agent misconduct, the injured athletes have alleged negligence by the unions in certifying the agents. In 1990, Dermontti Dawson and several other Pittsburgh Steelers sued the NFLPA for negligently certifying their agent and investment adviser, Joe Senkovich, Jr., who had mismanaged and stolen their funds. The court held that any state law negligence claim against the union was preempted by federal labor law. In order to recover, the Court held that the players would have to show that the NFLPA had actual knowledge of Senkovich's dishonesty and had failed to decertify him nonetheless. In 2006, several NFL players brought a similar suit against the union after investment manager Kirk Wright defrauded them out of $20 million. The players claimed that Wright had multiple liens against him at the time the NFLPA certified him and that the union was therefore liable. The NFLPA responded with a countersuit, arguing that the players were in breach of the union contract which states that the NFLPA does not endorse any of the registered financial advisers. The case was later dropped. Wright was convicted in 2008 of multiple financial crimes and committed suicide in prison while awaiting sentencing.

D. In Focus: Drafting the "Rep K"

Given the background in the previous three sections, the importance of the representation agreement in modifying the background rules of agency law should be evident. The representation

---

12. See Rule 3(B) of the NFLPA's "Regulations Governing Contract Advisors" for a complete list of prohibited actions.

agreement—or "Rep K," as it is commonly called in the industry[13] —is the most important agreement that an attorney/agent will draft throughout his relationship with a client. The representation agreement is between the athlete and the agent and includes basic terms, such as the scope and term of the relationship and the commissions and other compensation the agent is entitled to receive. As we will discuss in more detail, representation agreements may contain numerous other clauses detailing many aspects of the player-agent relationship. This section provides an overview of the various clauses, as well as important considerations for an agent or agent's attorney in negotiating each clause.

Threshold Concerns

In drafting the representation agreement, the parties must first decide whether they will abide by the form of a letter agreement or a more complete "full form" contract. The agent's general preferences will be to keep the agreement as short as possible, while creating a document that nonetheless contains all of the relevant terms. (Sample "forms" are available in the Teacher's Manual, as "exemplars.")

Once the form of the agreement has been considered, the agent's attorney must next begin the drafting of the legal document. While drafting, the agent's attorney should be sensitive to the concerns of the athlete, carefully choosing which subjects and/or clauses to include at the beginning of the agreement, to induce the athlete to continue reading. To that same end, the attorney should also use straightforward, "layperson's" language whenever possible, so that the athlete and his family can read and understand the document.

The Introductory Paragraph

In a letter agreement, the introductory paragraph should make clear that the remainder of the agreement will set forth the understanding between the agent and the athlete with respect to the management of certain later-defined business opportunities and matters. The introductory paragraph also should anticipate an acknowledgement at the end of the agreement that the athlete will, before he or she signs the agreement, "have read and understood the agreement in its entirety." The acknowledgement should also warn the athlete, preferably in all capital letters, that if he has any questions about his rights or duties under the agreement, he should have the contract reviewed by his own personal attorney. If the athlete is a first-time professional, then the introductory paragraph should also include warning language at the beginning of the agreement, such as: "You will lose amateur eligibility if you sign

---

13. "K" is a common legal shorthand for "contract."

this contract or have any other oral or written contract with an agent."[14]

By laying out these understandings at the beginning of a representation agreement, an athlete reading the agreement will be on notice that he is entering into a binding agreement, and that he should read no further if the athlete wants to have a personal attorney represent him. Putting such an understanding at the beginning of an agreement will help the agent enforce the agreement if, after the fact, the athlete claims that he did not understand what he was signing or that the agent tricked him into signing a contract without having the opportunity to review it with an attorney.

Scope of Representation Agreement

The next substantive paragraph will oftentimes define the "scope" of the representation for purposes of off-field or off-court endorsement and merchandising opportunities.

In that regard, in defining the opportunities and activities with respect to which the scope of the representation agreement will cover, the attorney for the agent will try to draft as broad a clause as possible. In other words, the attorney for the agent will attempt to describe "all incoming-producing opportunities and activities," as the scope of the agent's "exclusive" representation agreement with the athlete.

Of course, each of the categories of income-producing opportunities may or may not be the subject of an "exclusive" representation agreement; these are decisions that the athlete and his personal attorney need to make, depending upon each category of income-producing endorsements. For example, one agency may be preferable in the areas of licensing and/or product endorsements, whereas another agency may be superior in internet or multi-media opportunities. Similarly, the athlete may select a different agency for purposes of broadcasting or television opportunities and an architectural firm for help in things such as golf course design, if his career leads him in that direction.

What needs to be made clear in the scope of the representation agreement clause is whether the agreement will be "exclusive" as to each and every category mentioned therein and what "territory" the agreement will cover, i.e., whether it is worldwide or limited to a specific geographical area. What also needs to be made clear early on in the agreement is how contracts brought to the athlete's

---

14. This language not only clarifies any uncertainty the athlete may have about the effect of signing the agreement, but it also protects the agent from the type of contract nullification seen in *Walters & Bloom v. Fullwood*, discussed in Weiler, Sports and the Law, cited at p. 33, *infra*.

attention will be signed. Again, confusion in this area often can result in litigation that is easily avoided if care is taken in the representation agreement with respect to the authority that the agent will be given by the athlete.

For example, the best practice is that any contract submitted to the athlete must be signed by the athlete himself, rather than by the agent. A contrary practice which would permit the agent to sign on behalf of the athlete, whether by a power of attorney or otherwise, will often leave the agent's "authority" in question, if/when the athlete attempts to repudiate a signed endorsement agreement.

The question of ostensible authority, unless made clear in the beginning of the representation agreement, also can come back to haunt the agent if third-parties claim that the agent has orally committed to an agreement that the athlete chooses not to perform.

This question of such "apparent authority" was the subject of a recent lawsuit in which Richard Williams, the father of tennis players Venus and Serena, was alleged to have orally committed the Williams sisters to play in a "battle of the sexes" made-for-TV tennis exhibition. The Williams sisters' arrangement with their father was unclear, which allowed the question of whether the father's (alleged) oral agreement was binding upon the Williams sisters to go to a jury. The jury ultimately found against the Williams sisters but did not award any damages to the plaintiff.

That is why, in the initial representation authorization clauses, it is recommended that the agency affirmatively state that it shall not have the authority to bind or commit the athlete in any way, with respect to the income-producing opportunities to which the agent's representation will apply.

Merchandising and Endorsement Income

The next most important clause is a definition of that type of income that the agent will be able to commission or receive remuneration for obtaining, in the categories of representation defined earlier in the agreement.

In this clause, the definition of income needs to be as broad as possible on behalf of the agent, to include compensation "in any form," including, cash, stock options, futures, etc., or any other form of compensation "now known or hereafter devised," so as to protect the agent from disagreeing with the athlete over whether receipt of some form of compensation is commissionable or not. Again, a clear definition of the types of opportunities/categories, as well as the definition of the exclusivity or not with respect to each of these categories, will narrow the focus to the type of compensation the agent can receive. If "compensation" is thus extraordinarily broadly defined, the agent can thereby avoid a dispute over whether any monies paid to the athlete, for whatever reason and in whatever form, is commissionable.

The Compensation to Agent

Here again, the agent's attorney will want to draft as broad a clause as possible, with an eye towards commissioning any agreement that is "substantially negotiated" or orally agreed upon during the term of the representation agreement.

The agent's attorney will want to draft the compensation provisions in as broad a fashion as possible, to cover as many renewals of agreements that are either executed or "substantially negotiated" during the term of the representation agreement. The agent will want to get as high a percentage as possible for each of the categories of representation, in each of the geographical territories in the world in which the agent represents the athlete. The agent also will want to be specific about the form of compensation, in parallel fashion with the different types of income/compensation that are tracked in the paragraph concerning merchandising or endorsement income, so that the definitions of the two paragraphs match up precisely.

The question of compensation for deals that are negotiated but not completed during the term of the agreement also will need to be addressed carefully. Similarly, the commissions or compensation on agreements after the term of the representation agreement ends will need to be addressed. On the agent's side, of course, the attempt will be made to commission endorsement agreements forever, with an "evergreen" perpetual commission clause on any agreement finalized or substantially negotiated during the term of the representation agreement. Also, the agent will want to commission any "renewals, modifications or extensions" of deals sourced during the term.

On the athlete's side, the attempt to cut off the commissions as soon as possible, consistent with the date of the termination of the representation agreement, will be the push-back that the attorney for the agent should expect.

Questions of "quantum meruit" or hourly rate billing formulas also need to be considered, to the extent that an agreement is substantially negotiated during the term but not executed until after the term of the agreement expires. Disputes can be avoided if the subject of commissioning of renewals, modifications, extensions, etc., post-term of the representation agreement, are covered in the form of a pre-agreed schedule of the equivalent of "liquidated damages," so as to mirror the equivalent of a pre-nuptial agreement, as if anticipating the break-up of the "marriage" of the athlete and agent at the end of the current term of the agreement on a "no fault" basis.

Financial Services

In defining the scope of the agent's representation agreement, care will need to be taken as to how much, if any, of the financial services the athlete will require will be provided by the agent or his agency. This is a judgment call, which each agent has to address differently according to his own resources.

One school of thought dictates that the agent should want to control all of the financial services for the athlete so that it will be more difficult for the athlete to terminate the agent.

The opposite theory is that the agent should want nothing to do with the athlete's finances because he should not want to be responsible for reverses/downturns in investments that the agent may have recommended.

In any event, if financial service representation is agreed between the athlete and the agent, it should be the subject of a separate representation agreement. That way, any disagreements relating thereto will not impair the agent's ability to recover full commissions under the representation agreement—even if there are reverses in the handling of the athlete's finances, which the athlete might otherwise try to "set off" against commissions due under a "mixed" representation agreement, for example.

Expenses

In this clause, the attorney for the agent will need to take great care to specify who will be responsible for which expenses throughout the term of the representation agreement. The best practice is to delineate as many anticipatable categories of expenses as possible and to allocate responsibility for same.

On the other side, of course, the athlete's attorney will try to push-back as many representation-related expenses as possible onto the agent. In that interphase, the most difficult questions can arise in the following types of situations: who will pay for third-party professional service providers, such as attorneys and accountants, who provide services for the athlete at the request of the agent? The same question can apply to other specialized professionals whose services are needed by the athlete to promote his career, such as photographers, public relations specialists, and consultants, in specialized areas in which the agent himself is not an expert such as, multi-media or the "fantasy game" area of athlete endorsement.

On a simpler level, travel and telecommunication expenses arising out of the agent's performance of his duties should ordinarily be borne by the athlete. However, if/when the agent takes trips and/or incurs expenses (including cell phone and fax/overnight delivery expenses) without prior specific approval, a dispute can arise over the responsibility for same, unless it is clear in the representation agreement who will pay for that entire category of expenditures.

Also, a time schedule for reimbursement of all incurred and approved expenses needs to be agreed upon so that the agent can be paid in a timely fashion or, if not, earn a reasonable rate of interest on any outstanding amounts.

Internet Domain Names and Website–Related Costs

As a specific category under the expense heading, the athlete and agent should work out who will be authorized to obtain the athlete's internet domain name and who will pay for the registration of same. A clear authorization to the agent is important in this area, as well as in the area of constructing a personal website for the athlete. An additional paragraph clarifying who shall own any and all rights relating to the domain name and the website should be included in this section.

Also, in another section, the athlete should grant the agent the right to use the athlete's name, voice, likeness, image, etc., in connection with promoting the athlete, for purposes of income-producing opportunities. A tougher question in this area, however, is whether the athlete will permit the agent to use the athlete's "rights of publicity" in connection with promoting the agent and his agency with other prospective and current clients. This is particularly difficult in the area of providing financial services, where the SEC has specialized rules about promoting investment-related products through the use of celebrity testimonials which must be followed quite precisely if the financial services company is to successfully pass muster during the inevitable SEC audit.

Disclosure of Potential Conflicts of Interest Through Representation of Other Clients and Staging of Other Events

Here, there is a myriad of cases in which agents have been found liable for failing to disclose their self-interest in a deal in which their athlete has participated. Hidden referral fees or kickback commissions often prove to be the undoing of an otherwise healthy athlete/agent relationship.

Similarly, the failure to disclose "special benefits" that are being provided to one athlete, and not to another similarly situated athlete in the same professional sport, can lead to misunderstandings, if not made clear in the initial representation agreement.

Although the compensation clause in the representation agreement almost always binds the athlete to keep the agent's compensation "confidential," an agent's failure to disclose a potential conflict can often lead to a disgruntled athlete "comparing notes" with the other athletes represented by the same agent, who will try then to achieve a "most favored nation" downward adjustment in the compensation terms if/when the second athlete believes, rightly or wrongly, that the first athlete has been given an income-producing opportunity that would have been better utilized by the second athlete.

The same analysis can apply to the staging of events in which the agent can pick and choose among a number of his athletes for participation and guaranteed income streams relating thereto. In this category of "made for TV" events, for example, disclosure of the potential for "conflict," to all similarly situated athletes in the representation agreement is critical so that there can be no push-back if/when some of agent's athletes are chosen for the specialty event, and other athletes are not.

The "Term" of the Agreement

This is often a heavily negotiated clause of the agreement, depending upon the stage of the athlete's career and the leverage that the athlete has vis-à-vis the agent.

In general, on the agent's side, the term that is offered will be for as many years as possible, with "evergreen" renewal clauses, at the option of the agent, for the duration of the athlete's income producing career.

On the athlete's side, however, he should be counseled to go slowly, especially early in his career, by not committing to the same agent who may satisfy his immediate needs but who may not be appropriate for his career needs if/when he should "hit it big."

The same analysis should apply to the "term" clause that applies to the compensation clause so as to provide for a very clear payment schedule of commissions at the conclusion of the term. Post-term disputes over amounts owed can be avoided best by such clear drafting in the initial representation agreement. Also, protection against termination by the athlete during the term should be built in, to protect the agent's commissions. In that regard, a "notice and opportunity to cure" any alleged breaches of duty under the agreement will provide the agent with a waiting period during which he can attempt to rehabilitate a deteriorating relationship and firm up his entitlement to commissions during that same period before termination.

The clever agent will also begin to "substantially negotiate" new endorsement agreements during this "cure period" so as to attempt to lay claim to a commission on such agreements, even if they are finalized post-term, as described under the drafting of the compensation clause.

"Time" and Means of Payment of Commissions to Agent

A clause requiring all monies earned by the athlete to be paid directly to the agent is especially helpful here. As long as the athlete receives his monies "net of commission," on a timely basis, per the representation agreement, the agent will continue to be able to withhold commissions owed until final termination of the agreement.

Dispute Resolution/Mediation/Arbitration

Because the athlete/agent relationship is so high profile and easily upset by forces beyond the parties' control, it is often wise to include a "confidential" dispute resolution procedure in the representation agreement so that the athlete and agent can resolve their differences out of the public eye and, hopefully, continue to work together to their mutual benefit after the inevitable spat has subsided.

Specifically, in the dispute resolution clause, thought should be given to including a mediation clause, in advance of any binding arbitration, with the pre-selection of a mediator being a helpful palliative. Specifically, such a mediator may need not even be a lawyer, but instead a mutually trusted and respected person in the sports industry who knows how athlete/agent disputes usually get worked out to each other's satisfaction, on a confidential basis.

At the post-mediation arbitration stage, again confidentiality should be preserved. Also, limitations on arbitration-related discovery should be considered to control costs on both sides. A provision also should be considered as to the "finality" of the arbitrator's decision (or not). Additionally, a provision for the ability of the winning party to enter a judgment on the arbitration award in a court of the prevailing party's choosing should be considered.

Finally, the subject of costs and the disposition of same upon the conclusion of the arbitration proceeding should be addressed. In this area, the concept of requiring the losing party to pay the attorneys' fees for both sides will serve as a deterrent to either party going beyond the mediation stage to the arbitration stage, for fear of having to follow the British rule of "loser pays the winner's attorneys' fees."

Other concepts that need to be considered in this clause include the choice of law provision under the dispute resolution clause, which the agent will try to keep uniform for all of his athletes' agreements. Also, the procedure for choosing the arbitration forum and the rules of arbitration should be treated. The ability to seek an injunction in the event of the need for "emergency relief" should also be considered, if, for example, the agent is trying to "take the money and run" and cannot be otherwise prevented from doing so by the athlete through the dispute resolution process.

Chapter 1—Questions for Discussion

In light of the foregoing, consider the following "hypothetical situations," where an agent is recruiting a potential client. Based on the readings in this chapter, advise the agents about which actions are allowable and which are not. Students may also want to consider the companion text book Sports and the Law, Chapter 5, Sections b-d, in answering these questions. ("Exemplar" responses are set forth in the Teacher's Manual.)

In particular, which of these offers can be made without: a) creating a breach of fiduciary duty; b) a breach of NFLPA Player Agent regulations; c) the Uniform Athlete Agent Act; or d) a violation of civil or criminal law for Agent Top Cat, Agent Ziebart or MESCI's Agent?

A.   *Hypothetical No. 1—"Agent Top Cat"*

Matty Heisman ("Matty") is a star quarterback for Golden Eagles University ("GEU"). He and his family are conducting a "beauty contest" among various NFL agents to decide who will represent him when he turns pro, without losing his amateur eligibility status.

Top Cat ("TC"), who recently broke away from one of the largest NFL player representation agencies to begin an agency on his own after resolving his non-competition issues with his prior firm, offers the following items. In evaluating the offerings, consider that TC is also looking to work with a new investment advisory/financial planning firm that he can invest in or "control," as he used to work with such a firm which he partially owned while working with his prior agency. In that regard, Matty's father owns and operates such an investment firm, Heisman, Inc. ("HI"), through a family trust of which Matty is a beneficiary.

1.   A promise by TC to HI that, if Matty signs with TC, TC will use his "best efforts" to direct all of his NEW 2009–NFL-drafted clients (including Matty) to HI for a "referral fee" to be paid from HI to TC. (Note: TC does not intend to disclose this arrangement to his new clients (including Matty.)

2.   A promise by TC to use his "best efforts" to direct TC's CURRENT NFL clients to HI, for a "referral fee" to be paid back to TC, plus a further promise not to disclose to such clients TC's "referral fee" arrangement with HI.

[margin handwriting: "All of these still have conflict of interests and they cant fulfill his fiduciary duty if he is req'd to recommend one specific thing"]

3. A mutual promise by TC and HI to work exclusively, for reciprocal "referral fees," to recruit post–2009 prospective draftees to help TC and HI jointly recruit FUTURE NFL clients.

(Note: In this context, please note that different "recruiting rules" control "financial planners" vs. "agents" such as TC.)

4. A mutual promise by TC and HI to invest in each others' businesses post–2009, which fact will not be disclosed to current or prospective clients.

5. Also, because TC is an attorney who is "of counsel" to the law firm of NFLPA, LLC, TC offers Matty "below market-rate" legal services from that firm. If Matty uses that firm, TC will receive a "referral fee," which TC will not disclose to Matty.

B. Hypothetical No. 2—"Agent Ziebart"

Competing Agent Ziebart ("Z"), a former NFL owner, attempts to entice Matty and his family to come with his new agency by offering the following opportunities. While evaluating the items, note that Ziebart recently started his own NFL player representation agency after being removed by his family from his ownership position in his family's NFL team due to various charges of self-dealing and alleged Mafia/casino gambling connections.

1. Z offers to provide the services of his former team's (the San Francisco '99ers) NFL Hall of Famers/current Z-agents, to "coach" Matty in his last Bowl game and in connection with the North/South All Star Game by responding to any cell-phone and text message questions that might be initiated by Matty.

[margin handwriting: "extra benefit, before eligibility"]

2. Z promises that he will get the '99ers' current owner, his cousin, to draft Matty No. 1 in the upcoming draft, in exchange for Matty agreeing to sign with Z. In so doing, Z offers to act on "inside information," which he has learned through his son (who works for Z, but who is also a trustee/beneficial owner of the '99ers), that the '99ers do not intend to re-sign their current veteran QB for the next NFL season. Z also demands an "above-market" commission from Matty for arranging the "No. 1 pick" deal with his cousin.

3. Z also promises Matty a clothing line deal with Z's partially owned "Tony Baritone" signature line of men's clothing, including a "clothing allowance" which will pay, after the fact, for the Baritone-designed clothes that Matty will wear during the Heisman Trophy presentation.

[margin handwriting: "could be a benefit"]

4. Z. also promises that Joe South Dakota, his most famous former-'99ers agent, will present Matty with the "Golden Arm Award," at a ceremony "sponsored by" Z's agency, to be conducted just prior to Matty's post-season Bowl game.

[margin handwriting: "by increasing his draft stock"]

[margin handwriting: "also, don't know what the agents could ..."]

C.   *Hypothetical No. 3—"MESCI Agent"*

A Mega Entertainment & Sports Conglomerate, Inc. ("MES-CI") Agent, who works for a company with many different sports and entertainment related industries within in its corporate umbrella, offers the following items. While evaluating the opportunities, note that the MESCI agent owns a small percentage of "phantom stock" in MESCI. Each of the following offers is made on the condition that Matty must work "exclusively" with MESCI in each of the referenced categories.

1.   A guaranteed pre-draft training regimen at its wholly-owned subsidiary, the Performance Institute in Miami Beach, Florida, with former NFL/MESCI-employed All Star trainers.

2.   A broadcasting representation contract with MESCI's broadcasting division if/when Matty can no longer play NFL football.

3.   A guaranteed appearance in "Battle of the NFL Superstars," a made-for-TV turnkey operation, which is wholly-owned and produced by MESCI, for each of the first five years of Matty's career.

4.   SEC-registered investment advice through its wholly-owned SEC-registered investment advisory firm, MESCI Wealth Management Advisors, Inc., at no additional fee, as part of its representation agreement with Matty and not as part of a separate representation agreement with MESCI Wealth Management Advisors, Inc. (Note: A separate "disclosed" "referral fee" will be paid to Agent for such services.)

5.   A share in MESCI's Television Division's arm for any increase in ratings which produces increased profits that result from Matty's participating in games televised by MESCI's television arm, because of Matty's appearances in such MESCI Television Division's televised games.

6.   A partial ownership interest in MESCI's Football Division, for each NFL draftee that Matty sends MESCI's way from GEU, over the next 3–5 years, in the form of "phantom stock" commensurate with the amount MESCI's net profits increase as a result of such referrals by Matty, over the next five to seven years.

As you consider each of these hypotheticals, you should also consider how you would "modify" them, to bring the offers into "compliance" with all relevant rules, regulations, statutes, etc.

In so doing, your instructor should consult the Teacher's Manual for creative solutions to these agent-related legal issues.

Chapter 2

AGENTS & AMATEUR ATHLETES: UNDERSTANDING NCAA ELIGIBILITY RULES

At first glance, it may seem odd to include a chapter on amateur eligibility in a book entitled "Representing the Professional Athlete." In the United States, however, many successful professional athletes—including virtually all U.S.-born football and basketball players—use the NCAA as the jumping off point for a career in professional sports. Because many agents will attempt to cultivate relationships with these athletes during their NCAA careers, it is important that agents understand the relevant NCAA rules and regulations governing both the eligibility of their potential clients as well as the agents' own actions.

In the previous chapter, we first introduced the unique issues agents face while recruiting collegiate athletes by summarizing the Uniform Athlete Agent Act (UAAA), which has been adopted by the majority of states to regulate agents' interactions with college athletes. This chapter, however, will focus on the rules promulgated by the NCAA governing the eligibility of athletes to participate as amateurs, as well as how courts have reacted to agreements between agents and athletes that were in direct conflict with the eligibility rules.

This chapter will proceed in three sections. First, Section A will introduce the NCAA and its eligibility rules, including some of the more controversial applications of the rules. Section B will summarize some of the various legal challenges parties have made to the NCAA's authority to promulgate rules, including eligibility rules. Finally, Section C will turn to how courts have reacted when athletes and agents collude to break NCAA rules.

A. *The NCAA & Its Eligibility Rules*[15]

From its humble origins over 100 years ago, the NCAA has grown into a behemoth organization with some 12,000 member institutions competing in an average of 18 sports each. Perhaps fittingly, given the organization's current sources of revenue, the NCAA was first created to regulate the game of intercollegiate football. In 1906, intercollegiate football was responsible for some 15 to 20 deaths each year, and President Theodore Roosevelt (a former collegiate football player at Harvard) threatened to ban the game if university presidents did not come together and implement safety measures. The resulting organization of university presidents became the NCAA, and its first safety-promoting move was the introduction of football's forward pass.

One of the organization's first moves thereafter was to agree upon the principle of amateurism. Article I of the NCAA's Constitution clearly states the organization's amateurism ideal: "A basic purpose of this association it to maintain intercollegiate athletics as an integral part of the education program and the athlete as an integral part of the student body and, by so doing, retain a clear line of demarcation between intercollegiate and professional sports." In order to preserve this "clear line of demarcation," the NCAA members have agreed upon a complex body of eligibility rules laid out in Article 12 of the NCAA Manual, which is updated and distributed each year to member institutions. The "General Principle" laid out in Section 12.01 is that "only an amateur student athlete is eligible for intercollegiate athletic participation in a particular sport." Bylaw 12.1.2 then lists specific actions that will cause a student-athlete to lose his amateur status, including:

- Using his athletic skills for pay (directly or indirectly) in any form in the sport in which he competes (12.1.2(a));

- Accepting a promise of pay, even if such pay is to be received after completion of amateur eligibility (12.1.2(b));

- Signing a contract of any kind to play professional athletics, regardless of its enforceability or any consideration received (12.1.2(c));

- Entering into a professional draft after full-time enrollment at an NCAA institution (12.1.2(f)); and

- Entering into an agreement with an agent (12.1.2(g)).

Through a variety of other less-intuitive by-laws, in Article 12 and elsewhere, the NCAA also restricts the benefits a student-athlete may receive (both before enrolling at a member institution and

---

15. For readers seeking a more nuanced examination of the NCAA and the inherent tensions between its stated values and operations, see Chapters 9 and 10 of "Sports and the Law" by Weiler.

during enrollment), the promotional activities a student-athlete may participate in, and the employment of student-athletes during their period of eligibility.

Even casual observers of the sports industry are familiar with the most basic of the amateur eligibility rules listed above: Rule 12.1.2(a), which requires that no student-athlete receive pay for performing in an NCAA sport. Perhaps the most famous violator of this rule was Chris Webber, a member of the University of Michigan's "Fab Five" basketball freshman class of 1991. Webber and his classmates—Jalen Rose, Juwan Howard, Ray Jackson, and Jimmy King—led the Wolverines to consecutive NCAA Championship games in 1992 and 1993, and the freshman phenom Webber was named an All–American. A decade later, however, on the heels of a federal investigation that found Michigan booster Ed Martin had paid Webber and three other players over $600,000 during high school and college, the University removed the Final Four banners from the rafters of its gymnasium. In self-imposed sanctions, Michigan forfeited all 112 victories in which Webber or the other paid players—Robert Traylor, Maurice Taylor and Louis Bullock—played, promised to repay the NCAA over $400,000 in revenues received for participation in postseason play, and placed the program on strict probation.

More recently, former *Sports Illustrated* investigative reporter Don Yaeger has alleged, in his book *Tarnished Heisman*, that Reggie Bush, the Heisman-trophy winning tailback for the University of Southern California also violated Rule 12.1.2. Yaeger claims that Bush and his family accepted more than $291,000 in cash and gifts from Lloyd Lake, the financier of an aspiring sports marketing company, New Era Sports and Entertainment. Bush denied the allegations and, as of early 2009, the NCAA was still investigating the claims.

While there is a long-running debate over whether NCAA athletes should be allowed to accept pay for their services, the application of the "no pay for play" rule in situations like Webber's is pretty straight-forward given the current rules. Far more controversial, however, is the NCAA's strict application of rules to situations that could arguably be benign.

Consider for example NCAA rule 16.2.3, which bans "extra benefits" for student-athletes, which the NCAA defines as any benefits not "generally available to the institution's students." The logic of the rule was illustrated in the case of Dwayne Jarrett, a receiver at the University of Southern California. Jarrett shared an apartment with quarterback Matt Leinart during the 2005 football season, during which each player paid $650 month in rent to Leinart's father, Bob. Bob Leinart paid the remainder of the

$3,866/month owed on the lease. In June of 2006, the NCAA ruled that the rental arrangement was a violation of the extra benefits rule because Jarrett was receiving a benefit—a reduction in rent of some $1300 each month—that was not available more generally to USC's student body. Prior to the 2006 season, the NCAA compelled Jarrett to pay $5,352 to the charity of his choice as restitution for the improper benefits in order to regain his eligibility.

USC dealt with a similar, though perhaps more sympathetic, situation in January of 2008, when freshman star basketball player O.J. Mayo accepted a pair of courtside tickets to an L.A. Lakers—Denver Nuggets game from long-time friend Carmelo Anthony, with whom Mayo had been friendly since middle school. The NCAA ruled the tickets to be an "extra benefit" and required Mayo to donate the $460 face value of the tickets to charity before he could regain his eligibility. The same rule prohibits student-athletes from accepting free school supplies or free use of telephones and fax machines, complimentary tickets for parents to awards banquets, and rides from a coach or school employee (even to practice). At the most sympathetic end of the spectrum, a former Utah basketball coach was cited for a minor rules violation by the NCAA for buying then-Utah forward Keith Van Horn a 3 a.m. meal at a local diner the night Van Horn's father died in 1994. According to *Sports Illustrated*, Majerus bought the meal after delivering the news of the death to Van Horn, who then asked his coach to stay up with him until the player's morning flight home for the funeral.[16]

Another of the NCAA's controversial rules is found in Article 12.5.2 governing "Promotional Activities." The rule declares ineligible any person who, after becoming a student-athlete, either: (1) "accepts any remuneration for or permits the use of his or her name or picture to advertise, recommend or promote directly the sale or use of a commercial product or service of any kind"; or (2) "receives remuneration for endorsing a commercial product or service through the individual's use of such product or service." The NCAA's application of this rule has led to some odd restrictions, including the following:

- In 1985, Indiana guard Steve Alford was suspended for one game for appearing in a charity calendar put together by a school sorority.

- In 1994, Florida offensive lineman Anthony Ingrassi was told to stop penning a restaurant review column in the school newspaper, *The Alligator*, because it violated the rule.

16. See Rick Reilly, *Corrupting Our Utes*, Sports Illustrated, Wednesday, Aug. 6, 2003. In this context, consider two highly publicized 2008 NCAA bas-

- In 1996, Northwestern running back Darnell Autry, a theater major, was offered a non-paying role in the movie *The 18th Angel*. The NCAA initially ruled that if Autry performed, he would be in violation of one of the many rules falling under Article 12.5.2, in particular Rule 12.5.2.3.4, prohibiting the individual performance of a student-athlete in a commercial movie. After Autry won a preliminary injunction, the NCAA granted Autry a special waiver, based on his situation as a drama major, and allowed him to appear in the movie without threatening his eligibility.

- In 2002, the NCAA informed Colorado wide receiver Jeremy Bloom—who was also an Olympic moguls skier—that he would have to discontinue endorsement deals with ski manufacturers, a modeling contract with Tommy Hilfiger, and a regular television spot on Nickelodeon. Bloom had secured the deals through his fame as a skier, and, unlike Autry, was not a drama major in college. The NCAA refused to grant a waiver for Bloom, leading to the lawsuit discussed in Section B.

- In 2005, University of Southern California quarterback Matt Leinart temporarily had his eligibility revoked for telling the ESPN cameras "Sportscenter is next" during an on-field post-game interview. He was reinstated before missing any game time.

- In 2007, the University of Florida sent out hundreds of cease and desist letters to entrepreneurs creating and marketing merchandise bearing the name or likeness of its Heisman Trophy-winning quarterback Tim Tebow. The school wanted to ensure that Tebow's eligibility would not be threatened by his name and likeness appearing on merchandise produced by third parties.[17]

B. *Legal Challenges to the NCAA*

So far, this chapter has focused on introducing the NCAA's eligibility rules by providing real world anecdotes of their application. After reading through these anecdotes, most readers should not be surprised that the NCAA's rules have created a large amount of controversy, with parties attacking the rules on a variety of legal grounds. This chapter focuses on the three main types of legal claims that have been brought against the NCAA: (1) constitutional equal protection and due process challenges; (2) antitrust

ketball recruiting investigations involving two head coaches: Indiana University's Kelvin Sampson and Harvard University's Tommy Amaker.

17. Ironically, the NCAA and the University of Florida were not worried whatsoever about Tebow's eligibility or amateur status being affected by the officially-licensed No. 15 jerseys for sale in Florida's stadium shops. The NCAA bylaws expressly allow the school to sell its players' jerseys, so long as the players' names do not appear—even though the NCAA has (curiously) chosen not to

challenges; and (3) challenges based on the contractual relationships between the NCAA, its members, and student-athletes.

Constitutional Claims

Several parties have alleged that the NCAA's eligibility rules—
which they argue arbitrarily treat similarly-situated athletes differently—violate the Fourteenth Amendment of the United States
Constitution, which requires that no *State* shall "deny any person
within its jurisdiction the equal protection of the laws." In interpreting the Fourteenth Amendment, courts have held that private
actors will be considered to be the same as a State for purposes of
the Amendment if they are a "state actor." A state actor is defined
as an entity with power "possessed by virtue of state law and made
possible only because [the State actor] is clothed with the authority
of state law."[18] Examples of state actors include those persons
employed by the government—such as sheriffs—or private companies that are very intertwined with the government and govern-
ment-like work, such as privately-run prison companies or, as the
Supreme Court recently held, state high school athletic associations.[19] In order, therefore, to make out a Fourteenth Amendment
claim against the NCAA, a plaintiff would have to successfully show
two things: (1) that the NCAA is a "state actor"; and (2) that the
NCAA has denied persons equal protection under the laws.

In 1978, several Canadian-born hockey players for the University of Denver made this very claim.[20] As Canadian amateurs, the
hockey players had received room and board from their junior
hockey teams, compensation similar to what "amateur" NCAA
athletes receive. After the Denver squad—led by the Canadian-born
players—won the 1973 NCAA title, the NCAA retroactively declared the players "professionals" due to their violations of rule
12.1.2(a) by receiving payment "in any form" for performance in
their sport. The NCAA stripped Denver of its title and associated
revenues, and barred the school from post-season play for several
years. The school and the players filed suit in the District Court of
Colorado, arguing that they were being denied "equal protection"
under the laws, as players who could not have played junior hockey
without accepting room and board due to their limited financial
means. The court agreed that the NCAA was a state actor, but
refused to find that there was an equal protection violation, reasoning that while "the court is not oblivious to the less advantageous

oppose the use of college players' names
in a 2008 EA video game.

18. *United States v. Classic*, 313 U.S.
299, 326 (1941).

19. *Brentwood Academy v. Tennessee
Secondary School Athletic Ass'n*, 531
U.S. 288 (2001).

20. *Colorado Seminary v. NCAA*,
416 F.Supp. 885, aff'd, 570 F.2d 320
(10th Cir. 1978).

position in which a student-athlete without means may be placed by the effects of the NCAA regulations....neither the Equal Protection Clause of the Fourteenth Amendment [nor the Fifth Amendment counterpart]....guarantees "absolute equality or precisely equal advantages."

Two years earlier, in *Shelton v. NCAA,* the Ninth Circuit also ruled that the NCAA's eligibility rules did not violate the Fourteenth Amendment. After Lonnie Shelton had signed a contract to play for the American Basketball Association, the NCAA ruled that Shelton was ineligible to play for Oregon State University, under what is now Rule 12.1.2(c), discussed in section A, *supra.* Shelton, however, argued that the contract was unenforceable, and therefore the NCAA penalizing him for signing the contract was a violation of his rights to equal protection. The court disagreed, reasoning that "reliance on a signed contract as an indication that a student's amateur status has been compromised is rationally related to the goal of preserving amateurism in intercollegiate athletics."[21]

In *Wiley v. NCAA,* one of the NCAA's sub-rules against "extra benefits"—which specifically caps the amount of scholarship money a student-athlete may receive—also came under attack for allegedly violating the Fourteenth Amendment. In 1976, Wiley was declared ineligible to participate for the University of Kansas because, in addition to accepting his athletic scholarship (valued at $2,621), Wiley applied for and received a Basic Education Opportunity Grant (BEOG) from the federal government. The BEOG—which is only available to desperately poor students—was valued at $1,400 per year. The district judge hearing the case ruled that the cap on aid violated Wiley's equal protection rights because there was no rational relationship between the cap and the NCAA's stated objective of preserving amateurism. On appeal, however, the 10th Circuit overruled, stating that "the case does not implicate the right to a college education, or even to participate in intercollegiate athletics . . . unless clearly defined constitutional principles are at issue, the suits of student-athletes displeased with high school athletic associations or NCAA rules do not present substantial federal questions."[22]

While NCAA student athletes generally have not prevailed on due process claims, such a legal claim remained colorable—and student-athletes had a chance of winning—until the Supreme Court's 1998 decision in *NCAA v. Tarkanian.* In the landmark case, the Court held that the NCAA is not a "state actor" for purposes of the Fourteenth Amendment, primarily because of its national reach and scope, as distinguished from state high school athletic associa-

21. *Shelton v. NCAA*, 539 F.2d 1197 (9th Cir. 1976).

22. *Wiley v. NCAA*, 612 F.2d 473 (10th Cir. 1979).

tions. Since the decision, student-athletes have continued to try to make out quasi-equal protection arguments, but they have not prevailed. In 2001, for example, the NCAA declared Muhammed Lasege ineligible from participating as a member of the University of Louisville's basketball team. Lasege, a Nigerian citizen, had come to the United States via Russia to play college basketball, but he had arrived with the help—financial and otherwise—of an agent and some semi-professional foreign clubs. The NCAA ruled that by accepting travel expenses, room and board from these professional clubs, Lasege had "exhibited a clear intent to professionalize," despite that fact that Lasege had no other plausible way to obtain a visa to study in the United States. At the trial level, Lasege argued that the application of the NCAA rules was "arbitrary and capricious," and secured a preliminary injunction that ordered Louisville to let him play, and more importantly, ordered the NCAA not to penalize the institution for doing so, regardless of how the legal proceedings played out. On appeal to the Kentucky Supreme Court, however, the NCAA prevailed, despite the Supreme Court's odd assertion that "relief from our judicial system should be available if voluntary athletic associations act arbitrarily and capriciously toward student-athletes." In support of its assertion, the Court cited a previous holding that a high school athletic association, as a state actor, was obligated not to act arbitrarily or capriciously. No mention was made of the Supreme Court's ruling in *Tarkanian*. In subsequent cases, however, when a student-athlete attempted to rely on language from *Lasege*, courts have flatly stated that the standard laid out in *Lasege* is faulty.[23]

Antitrust Challenges

The NCAA—as even casual observers can observe—is a functional monopoly in most sports. Given its status, the NCAA is often subject to antitrust scrutiny and has proven to be vulnerable to legal challenges alleging Sherman Act violations. The Sherman Act, at its simplest, prohibits unreasonable restraints on trade. While there are multiple standards courts use to determine if a restraint is "unreasonable," the NCAA's actions are generally analyzed under the "rule of reason" standard. A restraint is considered unreasonable under the "rule of reason" analysis if its anticompetitive effects outweigh its procompetitive effects in a given product market.

Stated in the abstract, the test may seem difficult to understand for students who have not studied antitrust law. Therefore,

23. For example, when Jeremy Bloom (whose case will be discussed shortly) claimed that the NCAA's actions towards him were arbitrary and capricious—and cited the *Lasege* case for support—the argument was flatly rejected on grounds that the NCAA, post-*Tarkanian*, is not a state actor.

consider the following example. Imagine that the United States had one very large digital cable provider, with something like 60 percent of the market share. Now imagine, that there were four other, much smaller cable service providers that comprised the rest of the "product market." If two of the smaller companies wanted to merge, this would have anticompetitive effects, because there would be fewer competitors within an industry that already has a small number of players. However, there would also be procompetitive effects, because the merged company would be better positioned to compete with the dominant company. More consumers would actually be better off, because the dominant player would be forced to respond to competitive pressure. Therefore, on the whole, the merger would enhance competition, and survive antitrust scrutiny.

As you will see, the analysis is more complex when examining the NCAA's eligibility rules. Several NCAA practices have not withstood antitrust scrutiny, including restrictions on member schools negotiating television contracts[24] and restraints on the salaries member schools could pay to assistant coaches.[25] While restraints on the market for coaches and the market for television rights were considered unreasonable, the courts have been more sympathetic towards restraints on the market for players. While acknowledging that restrictions may have anticompetitive effects, the Courts have almost unanimously agreed that the procompetitive effects predominate. The two most important of these procompetitive effects is that the regulations supposedly "enhance competition among member schools" and preserve an amateur brand of athletics, which enhances consumer choice by providing an alternative to professional sports.[26] As one appellate court reasoned when rejecting an argument that the eligibility rules violated antitrust law: "The NCAA markets college football as a product distinct from professional football. The eligibility rules create the product and allow its survival in the face of commercializing pressures."[27]

Perhaps the most famous antitrust challenge against the NCAA eligibility rules—and certainly the most relevant to a casebook on representing professional athletes—was the case of Braxston Banks. Banks played football at the University of Notre Dame, and after four injury-plagued years he decided to forfeit his redshirt season and declare himself eligible for the 1990 NFL draft. In preparation, Banks also signed with an agent, therefore automatically ending his eligibility under by-laws 12.1.2(f) and (g) discussed in section A, *supra*. When Banks went undrafted, he attempted to return to Notre Dame, but the NCAA refused to grant him eligibili-

---

24. *NCAA v. Board of Regents*, 468 U.S. 85 (1984).

25. *Law v. NCAA*, 134 F.3d 1010 (10th Cir. 1998). In this context please consider whether the NCAA's BC's "non-playoff" system should withstand antitrust security.

26. *NCAA v. Board of Regents*, 468 U.S. 85 (1984).

27. *McCormack v. NCAA*, 845 F.2d 1338 (5th Cir. 1988).

ty. With the help of Ralph Nader's Public Citizens Litigation Group, Banks sued the NCAA, alleging that the rules unreasonably prevented players from receiving advice from an agent or declaring themselves eligible for professional drafts. The Seventh Circuit majority ruled for the NCAA on summary judgment, finding that Banks had failed to define any anti-competitive effect on a given market. In particular, the majority focused on the consumer market for fans of athletics and found that the eligibility rules enhanced competition by offering an alternative to professional sports. At the same time, the majority refused to concede that there was a competitive labor market for college football players, or that NCAA members were "purchasers of labor," as the dissent claimed. Instead, it reasoned that "None of the NCAA rules effecting college football eligibility restrain trade in the market for college players because the NCAA does not exist as a minor league training ground for future NFL players...."[28]

Many observers of college football would beg to differ. At the beginning of the 2008 season, only four players on NFL rosters— Ben Graham, Michael Lewis, Say Rocca and Ulrich Winklder—did not play NCAA football, suggesting that the NCAA is indeed the *only* "minor league training ground for future NFL players."[29] As major sports revenues have risen, some courts have grown more and more skeptical of the NCAA's amateur brand, and have shown a willingness to view the NCAA with a more critical eye. The dissenting opinion in *Banks*, for example, not only considered NCAA members to be "purchaser of labor," but also reasoned that the no-agent, no-draft rules allowed colleges to "squeeze out of their players one or two more years of services." Perhaps it was out of fear of coming before a critical court that the NCAA settled its most recent antitrust lawsuit. In the class action suit of *White v. NCAA*, four former players challenged the same cap on financial aid that *Wiley* challenged on equal protection grounds. The players argued that their "full athletic scholarships" did not actually cover the full costs of attending the member institutions, and that players coming from poor backgrounds were therefore forced to live below the poverty level while attending school. In January of 2008, the NCAA reached a monumental settlement estimated at $228 million, whereby the NCAA would provide back payment to effected football

---

28. Given the low graduation rates of student-athletes at the so-called college "football factories," as well as the "clustering" of "cake courses" that virtually entire football teams take at such schools which was chronicled in a late-2008 series of articles in USA Today, the frequently revisited proposition that these college athletes, who help bring millions of dollars into their universities' coffers, should be "paid to play," may indeed finally gain some meaningful momentum within NCAA circles.

29. As a counterargument, the NCAA estimates that less than 2% of senior football players at NCAA institutions (all divisions) will be drafted by the NFL, suggesting that the vast majority of NCAA football players are not pre-professionals.

and basketball players, and provide future funding to member institutions to help close the gap between the maximum scholarship amount and the cost of attending an institution for poor athletes. While some have questioned whether the settlement will truly benefit a significant number of athletes, the mere fact that the NCAA settled suggests a possible shift in the way courts—and the public—view antitrust challenges to the NCAA.

Contract–Based Challenges

Throughout our discussion of the constitutional and antitrust challenges against the NCAA, there was a consistent theme: courts have generally been reluctant to impose their judgment on the private, contractual relationship among the NCAA, its members, and student-athletes. By alleging a breach of those private contracts, student-athletes have provided a way for courts to overcome those concerns. Generally, there are two contracts that serve as the basis for the NCAA's organization: (1) the contractual relationship between the member institutions of the NCAA, who obligate themselves to adhere to the NCAA rules and subject themselves to the NCAA's regulation; and (2) the scholarship contract each athlete signs with a member institution, which among other things, subjects the athletes to the eligibility rules of the NCAA.

Easily the most famous recent contract-based claim was brought by Jeremy Bloom, the Olympic skier and Colorado football player mentioned in Section A, *supra*. In the spring of 2002, the NCAA ruled that Bloom would be ineligible to participate in intercollegiate football that fall, due to the various endorsement deals already discussed. Bloom challenged the NCAA's ruling, alleging that the contract between the NCAA and its members allowed him to receive remuneration from a professional sport other than the amateur sport in which he participated. In particular, Bloom reasoned that if the NCAA rules permitted professional baseball players (like Drew Henson and Chris Weinke) to accept the traditional renumeration for participating in their sports (a signing bonus and a salary) and remain eligible in other sports, then he should be allowed to accept the traditional renumeration for athletes in his sport (endorsements from skiing companies). Crucially, he claimed that as a third-party beneficiary to that contract, he had legal grounds for a breach of contract claim.[30]

At trial, the court held that Bloom and other NCAA athletes were indeed third-party beneficiaries of the contractual relationship

---

30. Bloom also argued that the application of the "promotional activities" rule was arbitrary and capricious (an argument that the court rejected out of hand, writing that since the Supreme Court's ruling that the NCAA was not a state actor, adherence to the NCAA rules does not implicate the 'state action' necessary to trigger a civil rights claim) and that it was an unreasonable restraint on trade.

between the NCAA and its members (including the NCAA's constitution, bylaws and regulations). The court failed to find, however, that the NCAA had breached the contract. On appeal, the majority agreed, reasoning that "in our view, when read together, the NCAA bylaws express a clear and unambiguous intent to prohibit the student-athletes from engaging in endorsements and paid media appearances."[31] The court went on to say that it could not "disregard the clear meaning of the by-laws simply because they may disproportionately affect those who participate in individual professional sports." The decision suggested that courts will strictly interpret the NCAA eligibility rules going forward, particularly those prohibiting any commercial or promotional activities by student-athletes. Ironically, however, just three years after the Colorado Court of Appeals handed down its *Bloom* decision in 2004, the NCAA membership was considering allowing member schools to profit from the commercial use of its athletes name and likeness. Historically, the NCAA has not allowed commercial sponsors of member schools to use the name or likeness of any current student-athlete. Under Proposal 2007–26, however, sponsors would be able to use game footage, audio, and photos of current athletes in advertisements, with proceeds going to the member institution. It is unclear whether the adoption of such a rule would call into question the "unambiguous intent" of the NCAA to "prohibit student-athletes from engaging in endorsements" cited in *Bloom*.

C. Judicial Reactions to Controlling the Relationship Between Agents and NCAA Athletes

The previous sections have examined, in some detail, what happens to an athlete's relationship with the NCAA when the athlete breaks the organization's eligibility rules. This section turns to another question that is probably more important to agents: what happens to the legal relationship between an agent and an athlete, when their relationship causes an athlete to break NCAA eligibility rules? The question can be restated more simply as "Is a contract between an agent and a student-athlete holding himself out as an amateur enforceable?" The answer, as this section will discuss, is "It depends."

In the case of *Walters v. Fullwood*, for example, the District Court for the Southern District of New York refused to honor a post-dated representation agreement between Auburn running back Brent Fullwood and agents Norby Walters and Lloyd Bloom. Walters and Bloom had induced Fullwood to sign the contract while

31. *Bloom v. NCAA*, 93 P.3d 621 (Colo. App. 2004).

still an amateur by paying him $4,000 upon signing and $4,000 during the course of his final football season. Upon completing his eligibility, however, Fullwood refused to honor the contract and defected to another agent before the draft. Walters and Bloom sued Fullwood for breach of contract, seeking recovery of the commissions they would have earned on Fullwood's first professional contract. The court refused, however, to enforce the contract on grounds that it was against public policy. In an opinion that generally lauded the amateurism ideals, the court reasoned that "the agreement reached by the parties here ... represented not only a betrayal of the high ideals that sustain amateur athletic competition as a part of our national educational commitment; it also constituted a calculated fraud on the entire spectator public."[32]

Subsequent rulings on the same issue have struck a very different tone. For example, another "client" of Walters and Bloom was Ron Harmon of the University of Iowa. Harmon signed a post-dated representation with Walters and Bloom while still a student, and immediately received a $2,500 "loan" along with small monthly payments. When Harmon attempted to void the representation agreement on public policy grounds, the arbitrator John Culver reasoned that even though the contract violated the NCAA rules, that was not illegal, and therefore irrelevant. Culver did, however, go on to declare the contract void under some of the NFLPA regulations discussed in the previous chapters.

Chapter 2—Questions for Discussion

In light of the foregoing, please consider the following "hypotheticals" which can be considered in group negotiating and drafting sessions. (Per usual, "exemplar responses" and sample Class Plans are included in the Teacher's Manual.)

A. *Hypothetical No. 1*

1. Re: Chris Weinke/Drew Henson/"Darnell Autry Exception"

Consider the following hypothetical, in light of the relevant case law and NCAA regulation-related materials that you have read in Chapter 2. As counsel to Henson/Weinke, what are the "do's and don'ts" if they want to maintain their NCAA amateur eligibility? Please cite the relevant cases/NCAA regulations/precedents in support of your conclusion.

1. Could Weinke or Henson, while (permissibly) getting paid to play pro baseball, but while also still seeking to maintain their college football eligibility pursuant to the NCAA's

---

32. *Walters & Bloom v. Fullwood,*
675 F.Supp 155 (S.D.N.Y. 1987).

"two team sports" exceptions, get paid to participate in a "summer theater" production for which they will be getting college credit from their college's Drama Department?

2. What difference, if any, would the following factors make in the NCAA revoking Weinke/Henson's eligibility or, if requested, granting a "waiver" as Darnell Autry received while playing football for Northwestern?

   a. What if Weinke/Henson wore Nike/Rawlings equipment during the "summer theater" production, while acting as baseball players in "The Boys of Summer," for which "endorsement" Nike/Rawlings paid the production company a promotional fee?

   b. What if the Minor League Baseball ("MiLB") games for which they are playing during the summer use the players' performances to promote their teams by, e.g., requiring the players/actors to wear specially made MiLB uniforms while performing?

   c. What if the MiLB team pays the players the standard "appearance fee" (approximately $50 per appearance), which is paid to all MiLB players for "community appearances," to meet with a local drama class to promote attendance both at the play and at the MiLB team's games?

B. Hypothetical No. 2. Re: Notre Dame's Tom Zbikowski Pursuing a Professional Boxing Career While Also Maintaining His NCAA Eligibility

What would you advise Tom Zbikowksi, former star safety for the Fighting Irish, if the following offers were made to him to pursue a "dual career" in professional boxing and amateur/NCAA football?

1. What if Tom wears specially designed "Everlast" boxing gloves during his professional boxing matches, for which the boxing promoter gets paid a promotional fee?

2. What if Tom wears tailor-made Notre Dame logo boxing trunks during the televised fight, for which Notre Dame gets paid a licensing fee? What if the coach of the Notre Dame boxing team treated Tom to a "free beer" at the senior bar to prepare him for his televised bout?

3. What if former Notre Dame All American Joe Theisman offers to broadcast Tom's fight "for free," and "donates" the value of his services to his alma mater out of his "admiration" for Tom's performances on the football field for the Irish? What if NBC, Notre Dame's primary broadcast partner, televises the boxing match and provides Tom and his opponent with an NBC-logo warm-up jacket, per

NBC's usual practice for televised fights, for use during breaks in the fight?

C. Hypothetical No. 3 Jeremy Bloom Revisited

What advice would you give to this high school senior/highly recruited football player, Jeremy Bloom, who also happens to be a phenomenal downhill skier, if he receives the following offers but wants to maintain his NCAA college football eligibility? Which of these activities would jeopardize Jeremy's NCAA eligibility in football? How could he participate with Team USA so that he could keep his options open for a possible spot on the US Olympic Team in 2008, while not losing his NCAA eligibility in football?

Please consider the relevant case law and NCAA regulations in providing your advice to Jeremy.

1. A top-ranked national "sponsored" ski team (Team USA) wants Jeremy to ski with them in the "World Finals," the travel to which in Aspen is paid for by Nike, the primary sponsor of the team.

2. Team USA also wants Jeremy to wear their "team uniform," which includes Nike and Under Armour logos, while participating in the World Finals and using the Nike/Under Armour gear, which is provided to all team members free of charge.

3. Prior to the World Finals in Aspen, Team USA also wants Jeremy to appear, in uniform, in a "team photo," which Nike and Under Armour will then have the right to use for promotional purposes if Team USA wins the World

As suggested in the sample Class Plan set forth in the Teacher's Manual, each "hypothetical" should be evaluated in light of the relevant legal standards described in this Chapter. "Exemplar" responses can then be shared with the entire class, to compare and contrast the "legal advice" that different groups within the class provide on a "confidential/privileged" basis to their "hypothetical" clients.

Chapter 3

THE ART OF NEGOTIATING IN THE "WONDERFUL WORLD OF SPORTS"

The first two chapters of this book introduced you to how agents "legally" go about obtaining clients. This chapter turns its focus to what agents spend the majority of their time doing once they have obtained athlete-clients: negotiating.

As we will discuss in some detail, there are as many negotiating styles as there are successful negotiators, and the best agents will tailor their negotiating strategies and tactics to the given situation. In particular, there are two general categories of negotiation that demand separate techniques: negotiating *with* clients and negotiating *on behalf of* clients. This chapter will begin by introducing some basic negotiation vocabulary and frameworks, and then turn to each type of negotiation in turn, providing a negotiation hypothetical for students to practice in each situation.

Throughout this book, you will be asked to consider which "negotiating style" best suits a given "hypothetical" set of athlete-representation facts. You will also repeatedly need to decide when a "pre-litigation-voice" will become necessary to best represent the interests of your athlete-client.

A. An Introduction to Negotiation Terminology

While this book does not intend to provide an exhaustive introduction to the academic literature, students will find it helpful to understand some of the basic terminology and concepts that negotiators and scholars alike use to describe aspects of negotiations.[33] For some students, this may be review.

---

33. Students who desire a more detailed overview are encouraged to read either *Getting to Yes*, Roger Fisher, William Ury & Bruce Patton, or *Beyond Winning: Negotiating to Create Value in Deals and Disputes*, Robert H. Mnookin,

Consider a not-so-hypothetical negotiation between two parties: Matt Ryan and the Atlanta Falcons. Ryan, the No. 3 overall
pick in the 2008 NFL Draft and the first quarterback taken, signed
the largest deal ever for a rookie, valued at $72 million over six
years. He is now thriving as a potential Pro Bowler for the Falcons
but, in retrospect, without knowing about this (so far) "happy
ending," how might that negotiation have been carried out?

- **Positions**—Most two-party negotiations begin with a statement of *positions*, or specific outcomes that each of the
  parties wants. For example, Ryan's agent Tom Condon may
  have told the Falcons that Ryan wanted a contract for ten
  years averaging $8 million per year, half of which would be
  guaranteed money. The Falcons may have responded that
  they wouldn't give Ryan a penny more than the top quarterback (and No. 1 overall pick) from the 2007 Draft, Jamarcus
  Russell. This would be a statement of each party's position.

- **Interests**—Interests differ from positions. While positions
  are the things that people want, interests are the *reasons
  people want things*. In our example, Ryan may have an
  interest in financial security and in knowing that the Falcons
  franchise values his ability. The Falcons, meanwhile, have an
  interest in keeping the salary low to effectively manage their
  salary cap. Meanwhile, both parties may have *shared interests*. For example, the Falcons and Ryan are both probably
  interested in long-term stability and in signing a deal quickly
  so Ryan can attend all of the preseason workouts. Identifying
  shared interests early on in a negotiation can help set a
  conciliatory tone and remind both parties why they want to
  work towards a deal.

- **BATNA**—BATNA is an acronym that stands for "best alternative to a negotiated agreement." In simple terms, a party's
  BATNA is what he would do if he cannot reach agreement in
  a given negotiation. For example, the Falcons' BATNA in
  their negotiation with Ryan would be to sign the best free
  agent quarterback available or to continue to rely on a
  quarterback already on the roster and draft another quarterback the next year. The Falcons' BATNA also involves,
  however, the turmoil and fan outrage associated with failing
  to sign the team's top draft pick. Ryan's BATNA is also
  weak. If Ryan did not sign with the Falcons, his best alternative would be to sit out a season or holdout for a trade. These
  alternatives ensure that he would not be paid in the near-
  term and that he would endure intense media scrutiny and

Scott R. Peppet & Andrew S. Tulumello.
Many of the concepts and terms dis-   cussed in this section were introduced
by Fisher, Ury & Patton.

criticism. When parties to a negotiation have weak BATNAs, they are more likely to reach an agreement.

- **ZOPA**—ZOPA is another acronym, standing for "zone of possible agreement." The ZOPA typically consists of all of the possible deals that fit in between the two parties' BATNAs, a zone in which each party would be better off reaching a deal than not. For example, assume that Ryan were not a draft pick but a free agent, and Ryan's best offer from another team was for six years and $50 million. Now, assume that the Falcons have assessed all other free agents out there, and have decided that in order to get a quarterback comparable to Ryan, they'd have to pay $90 million over six years. The ZOPA in this situation would be any deal that would pay Ryan between $50 and $90 million for the contract term, assuming all other factors are equal. In the ZOPA, both Ryan and the Falcons would be better off reaching a deal.

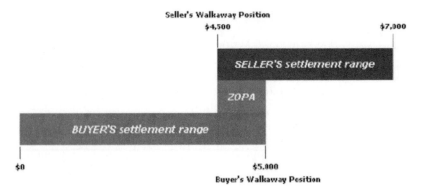

- **NOPA**—NOPA is a less common term in the academic literature, but the perceptive student can probably already guess the acronym's meaning: "no possible agreement."[34] Generally, it is used to refer to issues in multi-issue negotiations on which no agreement is possible.

B. *Negotiating With Clients*

Chapter one already touched upon the most obvious situation in which agents negotiate with clients: negotiating the representation agreement. Throughout the relationship, however, more informal negotiations occur all of the time, such as when an agent is trying to convince his client that a certain promotional or invest-

---

34. This term is taken from Michael Wheeler's "First Let's Kill All the Agents!" in *Negotiation on Behalf of* *Others* by Robert Mnookin & Larry Susskind.

ment opportunity is wise or unwise. Additionally, in the hyper-competitive market for sports representation, agents may find themselves negotiating to keep clients from ending the agent-athlete relationship and signing on with a new representative.

Preparing for the Negotiation

Before any negotiation with his client, a good agent must be prepared. First and foremost, he should know the person he is negotiating with, in this case, the client. What are his interests? What is his negotiating style? For example, is your client emotional or detached about business negotiations? Does he take things personally? Does he prefer to focus on the "big picture" or is he obsessed with details? What type of arguments are the most likely to persuade him? What is his BATNA?

It is equally important to evaluate your own positions and negotiation styles in anticipation of the negotiation. For example, if an athlete wants to renegotiate commission streams with his agent, the agent should think very carefully about his BATNA and at what point it makes sense to just walk away from the representation.

Next, it may help to think about the physical set-up of the negotiation. IMG founder and super-agent Mark McCormack discusses "the myth of the negotiation table" in his book *On Negotiation,* claiming that his "successful negotiations have rarely been conducted sitting around a table." McCormack argues that putting people on opposite sides of a table sends the wrong symbolic message, and that many negotiations would benefit from occurring on the golf course, in a restaurant, or at a sporting event.[35] This may be particularly true when the party in question is an athlete, as opposed to a businessman who may be more accustomed to formal negotiations.

Finally, the most important way to prepare for a negotiation is to anticipate it long before it occurs. In particular, agents who have long-standing relationships with clients should know that—especially if the client is incredibly successful—the client may begin to feel that the agent's commissions are unfair. For example, assume a rookie NBA player signed a five-year deal with Nike that tied compensation to the total number of shoe sales and the player's success in the league. In year one, the player may receive $1 million, of which 20 percent goes to the agent. This may seem fair, because the agent worked hard to secure the deal. Three years later—when the agent has done no additional work—the player may receive $5 million due to his success and the success of the shoe, and the agent would receive $1 million. All of a sudden, there may be resentment. McCormack describes this as "the paradox of

---

35. McCormack, pp. 87–89.

successful relationships."[36] By anticipating this negotiation, the agent can prepare the athlete for the contingency when the deal is signed, or the agent can structure the contract in such a way to ensure that walking away is painful for the athlete, weakening his BATNA.

Conducting the Negotiation

When conducting a negotiation, with a client or anyone else, it is often helpful to focus on interests instead of positions.[37] Positions of two parties are often incompatible. For example, there is no clear way to resolve an agent wanting to keep the same commission stream and an athlete wanting to reduce it, except for the painful "split the baby" approach. The underlying interests, however, may provide insight into a possible solution. The agent should, therefore, ask questions about *why* the client wants to reduce the commission stream and listen carefully to the answers. It may be that the client feels the agent is no longer working hard to secure additional deals for him or because the client feels he is being treated unfairly compared to other clients. The athlete-client also has an interest in not just the money he receives, but in his agent being incentivized to work hard and treat him fairly.

At times, however, even focusing on interests will not result in a satisfactory resolution. Sometimes the barrier to resolution will be differences between the parties, such as attitudes about risk, attitudes towards time, or forecasts about the future. With a little creativity, these differences can serve as the basis for a resolution if the parties can "dovetail differences."[38] A deal term that dovetails differences takes advantage of different expectations or beliefs to create value, giving each party what he values most. For example, if the athlete wanted to buy a new home and really needed that extra $1 million in compensation that the agent was set to receive, the agent could offer to forego the commission that year in exchange for a higher commission in subsequent years. Alternatively, the athlete might feel that the commission stream was unfair because the next year, based on performance incentives, the contract would be worth $15 million. The agent may believe that the contract would still only be worth $5 million, and the parties could agree to a flat commission of $1.25 million that would appeal to both parties.

Finally, when no resolution can be reached on a particular issue, the agent should think creatively to preserve as much of the relationship as is profitable. For example, if an athlete wants to

36. McCormack, pp. 168–170.
37. This was pointed out by Fisher, Ury & Patton in *Getting to Yes*.
38. This term comes from *3D Negotiation* by David A. Lax & James K. Sebenius.

terminate representation because he thinks that another agent has a better relationship with shoe companies, the agent could offer to represent the athlete in all categories other than the shoe category.

Chapter 3, Section A—Questions for Discussion

Renegotiating a Rep K: The Hypothetical Scenario

In light of the foregoing "tips" from Mark McCormack and other master negotiators, please consider the following set of "hypothetical" facts. Assume that Matty Heisman ("Matty") and MESCI (introduced in previous hypotheticals) have entered into a Representation Agreement that contains the following terms and conditions:

- **Exclusivity**—MESCI is Matty's "exclusive" marketing agent in the U.S. for all income-producing opportunities relating to his fame, skill or reputation as a professional football player. All such "opportunities" must be referred to MESCI prior to final execution of a contract by Matty, after review of same by Matty and HI/his father re: the financial terms and conditions of the deal. Also, Matty is reminded by MESCI, in the case of each Agreement referenced below, to have his "personal attorney" review same, if questions remain re: how MESCI's Legal Department drafted the execution-ready Agreement.

- **Term**—The Representation Agreement is for three years, renewable at Matty's option, with a 30–day notice period at the end of the third year.

- **Commissions**—MESCI/Matty agree to a "scaled" commission schedule as follows: 10% commission on the first million dollars received in endorsement agreements per year; 5% on the second million and all subsequent dollars received by Matty per year. All revenues are paid directly to MESCI, which must remit all receipts to Matty, net of commission, within 24 hours of receipt.

Also assume that, as of the effective date of the Representation Agreement—which is the date the Agreement was signed and became effective—MESCI has succeeded in securing several endorsement deals for Matty. In particular, MESCI has secured the following deals:

- **Adidas Deal**—MESCI "auctioned" Matty in the "athleisure" clothing category, to the winning bidder Adidas for a five-year deal with the following terms: year 1—$500,000; year 2—$750,000; year 3—$1,000,000; years 4 and 5 to be negotiated at end of year 3, but with a base fee no less than $1 million/year.

- **National Bank of Ireland Deal**—MESCI has also finished "auctioning" Matty in the "financial services" category, and gets a five-year deal with National Bank of Ireland (NBI) with terms: year 1—$250,000; year 2—$500,000; year 3—$750,000; years 4 and 5, TBD, but not less than $750,000 with the goal to make Matty "the face" of NBI in the U.S. (but not yet the face outside of the U.S.).

In addition to the deals negotiated by MESCI, six months after the effective date of the Representation Agreement, Matty sources and executes his own deal, without any assistance from MESCI. The deal is in the "publishing/ literary" category to be an author/columnist for "S.I. for Kids," and commits Matty to write weekly columns/annual "kids books," with these payment terms: five-year deal: year 1—base $100,000 (plus guaranteed royalties of not less than $25,000); year 2—$125,000 (plus trailing royalties); year 3—$150,000 (plus trailing royalties); years 4–5 to be determined depending upon success of sales in years 1–3, but paying a total of at least $150,000 in base fees and royalties.

Finally, as Year 3 is ending, MESCI sources and has "substantially negotiated" a deal with EA Sports for a "Matty Challenge" video game. The only "material term" agreed to is: $150,000 base fee for year 1, plus guaranteed royalties of not less than $25,000/ year. Matty tells MESCI that he wants a multi-year deal, or no deal at all.

At the same time Matty decides to terminate MESCI's Representation Agreement, and informs the agency within 30 days of the 3–year anniversary of the Representation Agreement. Matty notifies MESCI that he is going to use his father as his agent to, inter alia, finish the negotiation with EA Sports, and negotiate years 4 and 5 under each of his other major contracts. Matty also wants his father to expand his NBI relationship internationally, into Ireland and beyond, or to cancel same, if possible.

"You Make the Call"

As attorney for MESCI, make the best case possible for maximizing MESCI's commission streams, post-termination, under each of the Agreements referenced in the paragraphs above (Adidas, NBI, S.I. for Kids, EA Sports). In so doing, you can assume that the Representation Agreement commission clause entitles MESCI to commission all Agreements "executed or substantially negotiated" during the "term" of the Representation Agreement, as well as "any extensions, modifications, amendments, or renewals thereof."

As attorney for Matty, make the best case possible for minimizing MESCI's commission stream, post-termination, so as to maximize the amount of money Matty receives and, in turn, the amount of commission Matty's father's (new) player HI Representation (and Investment Advisors) Agency can earn, as "start-up" money for Matty's dad's new business that Matty plans to join when he retires.

In negotiating, keep track of those "tips" on negotiating discussed in this chapter that you used (or rejected) and specify the reasons therefore in developing your "negotiating voice."

Also, keep track of ZOPAs, NOPAs and BATNAs (if no final agreements can be reached) as well as any "pre-litigation" strategies you would consider using during the 30–day notice window. After negotiation with another student or group of students, draft a settlement agreement to memorialize the terms Matty and MESCI have agreed upon.

Set forth below please find some possible resolutions to consider in connection with finalizing the (draft) Settlement Agreement between MESCI/Matty Heisman and HI, based on the Chapters 1 and 3 Hypotheticals. (As usual, additional "exemplar" responses are included in the Teacher's Manual.)

Possible Resolutions to the Hypothetical

MESCI's General Counsel's ("Privileged/Confidential") Advice

For MESCI, as General Counsel, you could consider recommending to MESCI's Football Division Head that he should offer to represent Matty on a "non-exclusive" commission-sharing basis with HI, as HI "learns the ropes" from MESCI "jointly representing" Matty for the next three to five years, during which MESCI's commission stream would continue to diminish until another Rep. K "renewal decision" would be made by Matty/HI, depending upon the "value" that MESCI shows it could continue to add, during the effective "extension" term of the original three–year Rep. K.

Such a result would be a big "win" for MESCI, to be able to avoid litigation over its "evergreen" commissions claim, and to be able to say that it is continuing to "represent" Matty. Also, as a "sweetener," MESCI could offer to work with HI re: jointly pursuing future NFL high draft picks at Golden Eagle University, as Top Cat had originally proposed to do with Matty/HI.

Additionally, you might recommend that HI split out its financial advisory business from its agent representation business, so as to be able to take advantage of the less restrictive "recruiting rules" available to financial planners versus "agents." (In so doing, your ultimate "goal" would be to get HI to stick exclusively to "financial planning," and to be satisfied with only one client on the "agent" side of the business, i.e., Matty.)

In particular, MESCI could offer to represent Matty non-exclusively re: completing the EA Sports video game deal, where MESCI's expertise and "inside information" of the industry could prove invaluable for Matty. Also, MESCI could offer to "bundle" its other NFL quarterbacks with Matty in a proposed "QB Challenge" Video Game, to entice Matty to stay with MESCI non-exclusively in that category.

As to the NBI deal, MESCI could offer to represent Matty non-exclusively "outside of the U.S." by using its offices in Dublin and London to explore "on the ground" opportunities that HI could not exploit because of its lack of time/size/reach and connections. In so doing, MESCI could offer to "auction" Matty in the financial services/banking categories in Ireland and beyond.

As to the Adidas deal, MESCI could again agree to "phase out" its 10% commission over "the usual career-length" of an NFL QB on the current deal, but seek to represent Matty non-exclusively and bargain to get its full 10% commission for any "new money" that MESCI gets for Matty in "extension categories" (e.g., sunglasses), on top of the base fees for the "athleisure clothing categories" that have already been negotiated/agreed.

As to the S.I. for Kids Deal, MESCI could offer to have its Literary Division represent Matty if/when he extends his publishing career to additional "how to play QB" articles and books for more mature audiences, as Matty's own career advances. The same offer could/ should be made re: MESCI's Broadcasting Division, if/when Matty retires and heads into the broadcast booth.

In each of these offers, MESCI's goal would be to retain as many "income streams" as possible from Matty, and to "keep the door open" to expanding the relationship if/when HI falls flat on its face (as it most likely will!), even if Matty sufficiently "funds it," via an initial commission-stream split (and/or fixed-fee buy-out) in departing from MESCI.

Matty/HI's General Counsel's ("Privileged/Confidential") Advice

As General Counsel to Matty/HI, you could consider going back to Top Cat and Ziebart to reconsider "non-exclusive" representation possibilities, based on the offers made to Matty as described in the Chapter One Hypothetical. By so doing, you could "auction off" Matty among MESCI, Top Cat and Ziebart on a category-by-category basis, and drive down the commission-sharing arrangements with the eventual "winner." Also, by so doing, HI could find the right agency for the right category, and "learn the business" from the agency that is "best" in each "category" (e.g., Ziebart in the formalwear category, because of its "associations with the Tony Baritone Line of Clothing.) Also, joint-venturing with Ziebart would be helpful in the "inside information" category, given his continuing relations with the '99ers, etc.

In short, you would "spread your net wider," if you agreed to "joint representation" agreements with more than one agency, as HI attempts to grow its scope/reputation in the agent/financial planning business.

You could also consider offering another 30–day (or longer?) extension of the "Termination Notice" to MESCI, to see how many additional deals MESCI might bring to the table during that remaining "exclusive representation" time. In so doing, you would stipulate that any "new deals" so obtained would NOT be subject to the commission rates agreed in the additional Rep. K, but would be the subject of a renegotiated Rep. K. (Note: possible ZOPAs that might be at work here, for Matty/HI.)

You would also want to make sure that, during any such extension of the original Rep. K, all monies from sponsors were no longer sent directly to MESCI, but were sent to HI, to prevent MESCI from having the "leverage" of holding onto Matty's monies in the event of a NOPA/litigation outcome. If/when the Rep. K finally expires, you should immediately send notices to all sponsors indicating that HI is now "exclusively authorized" to agree on new deals or deal terms for Matty.

The separate "Financial Planning/Investment Advisory" Agreement that HI (or its separate affiliate) would offer Matty should also be "auctioned off" among MESCI and other "financial planners/investment advisors" who specialize in representing high profile athletes, as further enticement to get MESCI to lower its commission on the player Rep. K, if its "subsidiary" can continue to earn fees managing Matty's money through its separately SEC-registered (but MESCI-owned) financial services company.

Again, as noted above, please consult the Teacher's Manual for "exemplar" "settlement agreements" of this agent/athlete (pre-litigation) "hypothetical" negotiation re: the (possible) termination of the Rep. K.

C. *Negotiating on Behalf of Clients*

While much of the advice about preparing for and conducting a negotiation with a client also applies to negotiating on behalf of clients, the dynamics of negotiating on behalf of a client are different in several important ways. First, as an agent, you are no longer negotiating on behalf of yourself but on behalf of your client, as a fiduciary. Therefore, agents must follow all of the laws applicable to fiduciaries discussed in Chapter One. Second, many agents are more comfortable using additional bargaining tactics with third parties that they would not be comfortable using in negotiations with clients with whom they have long-term relationships.

As you will see, in particular, at this phase of negotiating in "the wonderful world of sports," the use of pre-litigation or "walk away" "threats" may may become necessary, in order to maximize the return on your client's investment in his professional sport.

Preparing for the Negotiation

When preparing for a negotiation on behalf of a client, much of the preparation is similar to the preparation already discussed. The agent should consider the other side's interests, BATNAs, ZOPA's and negotiating styles, and perform adequate research to prepare arguments in anticipation of the other side's actions. Additionally, however, the agent should ask another question: am I dealing with the right party? Sometimes, the answer may seem obvious, like when a client is negotiating with the general manager of the team that drafted him. But would it be better to be negotiating with the team president? Or the owner? Or all three? If an agent is seeking out endorsement opportunities for his client, he should carefully consider which companies he approaches and when. For example, while rumors that a client is engaged in negotiations with Nike could stimulate competing interest from some companies, it could also scare off competitors and inhibit competition. Before the negotiation even begins, the agent should ask himself, "Am I talking to the right person at the right time?"

A similar concern is the structure of the negotiation. An agent must decide if he should negotiate with one potential sponsor or team at a time, or instead conduct an "auction" of the athlete's services. McCormack refers to the auction as "negotiation's highest life-form," but cautions that "making an auction pay off for you demands near-total mastery of all the major elements of good negotiating."[39] While auctions can pit potential bidders against each other—and raise the price—they can also increase uncertainty and turn off potential bidders, who fear that they are just being used as "stalking horses" to raise the price.

All of these concerns will be affected by the athlete's current position in his career. Marketing students will be familiar with the four stages of developing a brand: introduction, growth, maturity and decline. These are also the four stages of an athlete's career. How negotiations—and deal terms—are structured should depend upon the athlete's position within his career trajectory.

At the Negotiation

Wherever the negotiation is occurring—at a table, or if McCormack is in charge, far away from a table—generally the athlete will not be present. The athlete's absence has several advantages: (1) it

---

39. McCormack, p. 173.

encourages candor on all sides of the table, as the agent and the team or company representative can speak freely about the athlete's positive and negative attributes without him hearing; (2) it allows the talent to spend more time focusing on his particular sport; (3) it allows both sides to engage in hard bargaining tactics that the athlete may not be comfortable with, and which could otherwise damage the relationship; and (4) it allows the agent to respond to any offer with the powerful phrase, "I'll have to discuss that with my client." This response prevents athletes or agents from hastily agreeing to anything and thereby keeps opposing parties from "winning" particular negotiating points and gaining momentum.

There are, however, times when it may be useful to bring the athlete into the negotiations. One situation is when the athlete has a personal relationship with the opposing party that could help smooth the negotiations. Another is only applicable to superstar athletes, who often have the ability—merely by their presence—to encourage otherwise savvy businessmen to make concessions they were not willing to make to the agent. As McCormack writes, "After all, it is one thing for the other side to tell me, 'Your superstar isn't worth the price you're asking.' It's another for them to say it to the superstar's face."[40]

With the athlete out of the room, however, negotiations tend to be much tougher, and there is disagreement over the utility of hard bargaining tactics. While McCormack's philosophy generally encourages agents to "think big" and not be afraid to make an "insulting" offer, refuse to respond to low-ball offers by adopting a patient "Buddha" approach, and/or "play hardball," other commentators worry about the agency costs imposed on athletes by such techniques. Brian Mandell argues, for example, that because there is so much media attention paid to player salaries and contracts, agents are incentivized to use hard bargaining tactics to simply achieve the highest possible total compensation for the athlete.[41] These tactics do not take into account other interests players may have, such as avoiding negative media attention (such as the kind associated with a holdout), playing in a city the player enjoys living in, or playing for a coach who is likely to help the player's career in the long-run.

Another commentator, Michael Wheeler, has argued that because both sides embrace hard bargaining tactics focusing on salary, most *successful* negotiations actually begin with a perceived NOPA.[42] Only after lengthy and costly negotiations do one or both

40. McCormack, p. 101.

41. Mandell, "Unnecessary Toughness," *in* Mnookin & Susskind, *Negotiating on Behalf of Others*, at 264.

42. Wheeler, "First, Let's Kill All the Agents!" *in* Mnookin & Susskind, *Negotiating on Behalf of Others*, pp. 255–56.

parties reassess their BATNAs and realize that there is a ZOPA after all.

A real life example of such a scenario occurred when Scott Boras was negotiating with the New York Yankees on behalf of Alex Rodriguez during the 2007 off-season. Rodriguez's initial contract with the Yankees had included three option years in 2008, 2009 and 2010 valued at $81 million, of which $21 million would be paid by the Texas Rangers (who had assumed the salary in a trade), assuming Rodriguez did not opt out. Because Boras believed that Rodriguez had a strong BATNA—that other teams would be willing to pay more than that amount for Rodriguez—he encouraged Rodriguez to opt out, which he did. After realizing that no other team was willing to pay nearly as much as the Yankees for Rodriguez's services—and that Boras had allowed his own relationship with the Yankees to deteriorate due to the hard bargaining tactics—Rodriguez himself contacted Yankees owner George Steinbrenner's son Hank to renegotiate the deal. After securing a 10–year, $275 million contract (which presumably could have been higher if the Yankees were still receiving $21.3 million from the Rangers) without Boras' help, Rodriguez publicly admitted that opting out was, "a mistake that was handled extremely poorly. It was a huge debacle." The week after signing his contract, Rodriguez announced he had fired Boras.

In Boras' defense, however, hard bargaining tactics often work. Rodriguez's deal was, in the end, the largest in the history of MLB, topping the previous contract of $252 million Boras had negotiated for Rodriguez. Interestingly, because Boras' clients are known to "sit out" if they do not receive certain signing bonuses following the MLB amateur draft, usually only franchises that are willing to pay huge signing bonuses draft his players.

When the Negotiation Fails

In the negotiation examples discussed above, the parties' BATNAs usually involved reaching a deal with a different athlete, franchise or company. Oftentimes, however, both parties' BATNAs in a given situation may be the same: litigation. Skillful negotiators generally seek to avoid litigation and arbitration because, as academics commonly say, they involve *uncertain* outcomes and *certain* costs. Litigation—and even arbitration—can be extremely costly, and usually if both parties are willing to proceed to litigation it is because there is (uncalculatable) uncertainty over what the outcome will be.

Arbitration, while generally more efficient than litigation, presents similar problems of uncertainty. As an example that may be familiar to sports fans, consider how arbitration works in the MLB. When a young player achieves the requisite service time in the big leagues, but he is not yet a free agent, the player is not required simply to accept whatever salary his club offers. Instead, the collective bargaining agreement provides that if the player and club cannot agree on a salary, then each party may submit a salary offer to an arbitrator, who will choose one of the two offers, based upon a set of factors including the player's performance history, age, and peer group salaries. Notably, the arbitrator may not "split the difference," a unique nuance that has led academics to describe such a process as "baseball arbitration." The nuance—which increases the risk of going to arbitration—was implemented to encourage the parties to settle on their own.

While litigation can be a weak BATNA, the *threat* of litigation can be a useful negotiating tactic, especially if the other party will find it relatively more difficult to bear the legal fees and other costs of a trial. Oftentimes, even if a party feels confident it would win at trial, the party may still choose to settle because it simply cannot afford a lawsuit or because settling will be more efficient. Because even the threat of litigation can be so powerful, agents need to be extremely careful in drafting legal documents that could later be litigated. Section D in this Chapter, at p. 55, "In Focus: Common Legal Drafting Mistakes," highlights some of the faux pas new attorneys should look for while drafting legal documents, in order to avoid litigation pitfalls.

IN FOCUS: NEGOTIATING AND DRAFTING A PRODUCT ENDORSEMENT AGREEMENT

Now you can apply all of the foregoing negotiating "theory" to the "practical example" of negotiating and drafting the athlete's first income-producing agreement—"the product endorsement agreement."

"Suitability" Clause

The key to drafting the product endorsement agreement is the "suitability" clause. In such a clause, the player agrees to use a sponsoring company's product during his professional play, in exchange for the company's providing him with "products" (which can include playing equipment and apparel that the player will agree to use/wear while engaging in professional competition) as long as he deems it "suitable for use."

For example, a golf or tennis professional will be offered a sponsorship endorsement opportunity to try a new or different golf club or tennis racket, as the player begins to come into the maximum income-producing years of his career. The choice between staying with his old brand of clubs or rackets versus trying out a new set of products will often be tied to the "psychology of success" that is imbedded in his many years of training and competing using the prior brand of clubs or rackets.

Yet, in general, the opportunity to "auction" the products market will require the player to be "indifferent" to the possible switch to different products, to avoid getting low-balled by his historical products-maker on the theory that the player will not risk decreasing his performance level in exchange for a richer endorsement agreement with new but untested products made by a competitor.

Thus, as a mid-career player approaches the renewal of his original equipment and clothing deals, he should provide his long-standing product partner with adequate notice that will allow the player the flexibility to switch, if so desired, so as to avoid an "automatic rollover" due to lack of sufficient notice either per the contract or per the past practice for renewals that the player and the products manufacturer have established.

During this "notice" period, the player should make it clear to his prior sponsor that, unless a new and improved playing product will be "tailor made" to his specifications, he will exercise his rights to seek other endorsement opportunities in a way that is consistent with the "right of first refusal" that is usually included in his original product endorsement agreement. The "auction" of the product category thus begins, and a "trial period" for all competitor's products should be set up at the earliest opportunity by the player's agent/attorney contacting all competitors and letting them know that a product change is available as of a certain date.

"Trial Period"

During the "trial period," the player will demand both from the current sponsor and any competitors, the equivalent of an RFP for new playing product specifications that would be issued to all members of the auction competition. The player should provide himself with sufficient time (at least 90 days) within which to test the new products in various settings, before ultimately committing to play the product. After the trial period, the player should also continue to protect himself by insisting upon a "suitability clause" that permits him to cease playing the product if/when he no longer deems the product to be "suitable for use" in his professional competition. The difficult part of crafting such a clause, however, is that the product manufacturer/sponsor will want to receive assurances that, once the product has been selected, the player will continue to play the product in professional competition unless some "defect" in the product is revealed that was not detectible during the "trial period."

Escape Clauses

Conversely, the player will want to leave himself with sufficient "escape clauses" that will permit him to return to his prior products if/when the new products result in sub-par performance, for no reason other than familiarity with the prior products. Thus, the drafting of the "suitability clause" will range from an absolute requirement that the player must play the new product, regardless of results, to a much softer requirement that the player can return to playing his prior product or even a competitor's product, for which the new product manufacturer will receive some negotiated form of monetary relief while it tries to "cure" any (alleged) "defects" before terminating the new agreement altogether.

In other words, a "high risk/high reward" strategy for the player would be to commit unconditionally to the "suitability" of the product, after the trial period, and leave himself with no "escape clauses" even if his performance deteriorates after the new agreement has been executed. For such an absolute commitment, the player can command "top dollar," because the sponsor can reliably put an advertising campaign behind the player's use of the new product, on the assumption that there will be no interruption in the player's (successful) use of the new product.

The "lower risk/lower reward" strategy for the player would be for him to reserve the right to stop using the new product if, in his "sole discretion," he no longer deemed it to be "suitable for use in professional play." Such an "escape clause" would decrease his monetary parameters with the new product manufacturer, but would also protect his performance downside in the event that the new product proved to be less successful for the player in competition.

A middle ground would be for the player to commit to use the new product "if it is deemed suitable in his reasonable or professional judgment." Agreeing to such a clause in the new product agreement will at least somewhat objectively define the contours of when the player can switch back to his old product (or to a competitor's product), so that such a switch must be based on a verifiable standard of "reasonableness," rather than the player's "absolute discretion."

Other Clauses

Once the "suitability clause" has been agreed upon, the rest of the product endorsement agreement can be negotiated to provide for all other eventualities that could lead to the player no longer playing the product during the agreement's term.

For example, the sponsor must protect itself against the player disparaging the product which he has committed to play, with a standard form of non-disparagement clause. Similarly, the sponsor should tailor a "morals clause" to anticipate a right to terminate that matches the player's history, if any, of non-conforming behavior. On the player's side, product "quality assurances" must be enforceable, lest the sponsor not supply adequate amounts of non-defective product. Also, product "tweaking rights" should be reserved to force the sponsor to fine-tune the product as the player commences a product switch in tournament play.

On both sides of the agreement, clear "limitation of liability" provisions should be agreed, in the event of a breach by either party. So, too, should a "dispute resolution clause," with "notice and opportunity to cure" be considered, to avoid a "race to the courthouse" in the event that the player shows up at a tournament intending to play a (contract-breaching) competitor's product, and the sponsor responds by seeking to enjoin such use with a "summons to appear in court" on the first tee!

Other clauses that must be incorporated into any new or renewed product agreement include "force majeure" and "injury/disability" clauses that provide for the "unforeseen events" that might preclude the player from playing the product due to "acts of God" or disability/injury interruptions of the player's agreed playing "term."

Finally, agreement must be reached on when and where the player must use or wear the contracted "products." In general, such an agreement should require the player to use/wear the products whenever participating in any professional event relating to the sport in question. The further requirement that the player must wear/use the endorsed product "whenever in public" can create a host of litigatable issues, as well as a demand from the player for extra compensation if he must wear/use the endorsed products "whenever in public" and/or when endorsing other non-competing product categories.

Possible post-trial period "compromises" on the "suitability clause" could include a pro-rated agreement to use the sponsor's clubs/racket for a minimum number of tournaments/events, for which a reduced fee would be paid. Also, in the golf context, a sub-agreement re:, e.g., certain selected clubs (e.g., the irons and woods, but not the putter) could be agreed, with an appropriate pro-rated adjustment built in.

In so doing, however, the sponsor will not want to dilute the effectiveness of the athlete endorsement by, e.g., permitting the player to opt out of using the sponsor's equipment in the major rounds of the major tournaments. Such potential "maximum exposure" for the sponsor will most likely result in a "must play" requirement that the player might resist because it is precisely at those same times/events that his "psychology of winning" might dictate reverting to his old/more familiar pieces of equipment and/or "lucky Sunday clothing."

The careful draftsperson will anticipate each of these eventualities in the post-trial-period term of the agreement, with appropriate "post-nuptial" types of walk-away provisions, with each side know-

ing precisely what the "cost" will be if/when the player intentionally violates a "must use" contractual requirement, under "game
conditions."

Conclusion

In sum, this entire area of contract drafting is where "knowing
your client" is paramount for the attorney representing the professional athlete, because anticipating a "worst case" reversion by the
athlete to non-required equipment should be clearly monetized in
the agreement and the "cost" of an intentional "breach" should be
agreed upon, in writing, by the athlete; after the athlete has been
encouraged, if not required, to seek the advice of his "personal"
(i.e., non-agency) attorney. Otherwise, when litigation inevitably
ensues, a "malpractice claim" could be brought after the fact, if the
athlete can claim that he (and his "personal attorney") did not
understand the "price" that the athlete would have to pay for
violating a mandatory "suitability clause," at a critical time, in a
critical tournament/event.

Chapter 3, Section D—Questions for Discussion

Please use all of these drafting "tips" in considering the
following "hypothetical." As usual, "exemplar" responses are included in the Teacher's Manual.

1. Negotiating a Product Endorsement Agreement: The Hypothetical "Product Suitability" Scenario

In this hypothetical, you should assume the following facts: A
top–30 PGA player ("Player"), who is in his early 30s, is coming up
for a renewal on his golf clubs/bag and clothing/shoe deals. He has
been with the same club manufacturing company since he began
playing golf as a kid. He is very comfortable with these clubs, as
well as the accompanying bag and clothing/shoe deal, but he is
being paid "below market" money because XYZ knows that he and
his agent are not inclined to conduct an auction and go to the
highest bidder when he comes up for renewal at year's end.

Assume further that the PGA Tour is ending as mid-November
approaches and that Player must renew his XYZ deal (or not) by
January 1.

Player has been approached by a new club manufacturing
company (ABC), whose clubs are now played by a few low-ranking
PGA Tour players. ABC is a new start-up company, which is
privately held. ABC is offering to make Player its "poster child" in
a new advertising campaign/media blitz, as of January 1 of the next
year, culminating with Player playing its ABC clubs, carrying its
ABC bag, and wearing its "head to toe" ABC-logoed clothing and
shoes in the season-opening Dubai Classic to which Player has been
invited to play with the other top players in the world.

ABC is willing to offer Player an above-market deal, including
an equity share in the ABC company, if Player will sign "exclusive-

ly" with ABC, for a multi-year term. ABC is also willing to allow Player to have a six-week "trial period" from mid-November through December 31 during which Player can test the ABC clubs and fine-tune them to fit his specifications, before agreeing to play the ABC clubs at the Dubai Classic. After January 1, however, Player must irrevocably commit to play the ABC clubs so that ABC can roll out its aggressive advertising campaign/media blitz.

The key to the negotiation is the "suitability clause" in which Player must commit to play the ABC clubs after January 1, if ABC makes the clubs "suitable for use" in PGA Tour play. Player wants to change this clause to require that the clubs be suitable for use "in his sole discretion."

Other issues that should be considered in negotiating the hypothetical and drafting the "key clauses" include the following:

1. The "morals clause," given Player's (well-documented) history of public drunkenness, which has limited his ability to obtain major endorsement deals in other categories. In that regard, consider whether an arrest is sufficient to void the deal or whether a conviction (or "nolo" plea) is necessary, either for a misdemeanor or a felony.

2. The "force majeure clause," given the fact that the Dubai Classic has been targeted by terrorists for a possible attack. Player is particularly nervous about terrorist attacks and wants to be able to invoke the clause in the event that he feels it is unsafe to play there. However, ABC does not want Player to be able to invoke the "force majeure clause" based on a claim that he is nervous over changing clubs for the first time at the Classic, or because of self-imposed limitations related to his alcohol consumption.

3. The "limitation of liability clause," in which Player wants to limit his exposure if he begins to play with ABC's clubs after January 1, but then realizes that he is not able to be competitive with them on the Tour.

4. The "alternative dispute resolution" clause, which Player wants in order to "confidentially" resolve away disputes "out of court," but which ABC does not want because it will need to seek injunctive relief in court if Player suddenly appears at a PGA Tour event playing his old XYZ clubs.

5. Compensation and bonuses—what payment, if any, should be made to Player during his trial/test period? What separate deal, if any, should be struck for a partial clothing/shoe or golf bag deal? What bonuses should be paid for winning a Major tournament or a PGA Tour event? Should Player's caddy be included in the ABC clothing and/or shoe deal?

6. "Term" of agreement—Here, both sides need to consider the "four stages" of Player's career in which his best income-producing years on Tour should be forthcoming in the next three to five years. At the same time, both parties will want an "out" if Player plays significantly better or worse than he has been playing over the last few years when he has been consistently ranked in the Top 30 on the PGA Tour list with a few wins in non-Major events and a number of close finishes in Major events.

You can now use this "hypothetical" to conduct a negotiation/drafting exercise with one Group representing ABC and the other Group representing Player. Keep track of the ZOPAs, NOPAs and BATNAs of each Group, and draft a product endorsement agreement—or at least the key clauses—memorializing the deal. Remember that you are drafting a legal document, and therefore that word choice and punctuation are extremely important. When drafting, consider carefully whether the language you have chosen clearly anticipates every contingency, and whether the language will carry with it a clear legal meaning to any judge interpreting it. With permission, you may use the "exemplar" Product Endorsement Agreement found in the Teacher's Manual as a reference, but not as a template.

Students may find the preceding "In Focus: Negotiating and Drafting a Product Endorsement Agreement" and the following "In Focus: Common Legal Drafting Mistakes" helpful in drafting this agreement and other agreements throughout the book.

Also, as usual, the Teacher's Manual will provide helpful hints and "Exemplar" responses to the hypothetical last patterns.

IN FOCUS: COMMON LEGAL DRAFTING MISTAKES

Many novice legal drafters make similar rookie mistakes when crafting legal documents for the first time. Below is a list of the most common drafting mistakes, to help you avoid them as you begin to draft the professional athlete's first "product endorsement agreement," and other agreements throughout this book.

Definitions

1. Avoid Using Undefined / Ambiguous Terms
   - Ex. If Player is *dissatisfied* with clubs . . .
     o Instead use: If Player, in his sole discretion, determines that clubs are not suitable for his use . . .
   - Ex. If Golfer *approves* the proposed advertising materials.
     o Instead use: If Golfer grants his written authorization . . .

2. Be Wary of Overly Broad/Narrow Definitions
   - Complications may arise if a key term (ex. product category) is inadvertently defined too broadly/narrowly.
3. Use Defined Terms Clearly and Consistently
   - Capitalize defined terms to accord them their intended meanings.
4. Be Cautious When Using Legal Terms of Art
   - Some terms have legal meanings that may be different from their everyday meanings, so be careful when using these terms.
   - Ex. "Terminate" and "void" have separate and distinct legal meanings.

Grant/Reservation of Rights

5. Synchronize Grant/Reservation of Rights
   - Within the same section of the agreement, clearly delineate the "grant" and the "reservation" of rights in different clauses with the grant preceding the reservation.
6. Cover Future Contingencies / Categories
   - Ex. Except those (narrow) "product category" rights granted to ABC, Golfer should reserve all other rights to exploit his marketing rights in any other "product categories" and in any form of media, including "all forms of media now known or hereafter devised."
   - How does the agreement enable the parties to extend the grant of rights so ABC can create a new line of products or shoes/clothing that is "substantially similar" to previously approved product/apparel?
   - Are rights transferable? Do they pass to Golfer's heirs and assigns?

Termination

7. Which Breaches Are "Material?"
   - Indicate those clauses/sections that, if violated, would result in material breach.
   - Can some breaches result in immediate termination, while others require notice and time to cure?
8. Alternative Means of Termination
   - Can Golfer opt out or renegotiate if his ranking increases significantly or if he wins another Major?
   - Can ABC terminate if Golfer loses his PGA Tour card, disparages the product, or acts in a manner that dramatically

decreases the value of Golfer's "marketability"/rights of publicity?

- Can either party terminate if Player keeps (arbitrarily) rejecting ABC's "test products"?

Remedies / Post–Termination Rights

9. How Are Damages Determined?

- How are they calculated? Is there a (mutual?) limitation of liability? Are consequential/punitive damages available?

- Are different remedies available for various classes of breaches?

10. Account for Post–Termination Rights

- What happens to unsold merchandise, or works in production?

- Will existing revenue streams continue? If so, for how long, and on what "profit split" basis?

Other Considerations

11. Internal Consistency / References

- Ex. An ADR clause with a mandatory waiting period before initiating litigation / arbitration may conflict with a right to seek injunctive relief as stated in a separate clause.

   o Solve this problem by including a carve out for court-ordered injunctive relief within the ADR clause.

- Internal citations referring back to particular clauses can ensure internal consistency.

12. Consider Timing

- When must the parties exercise their rights or fulfill their obligations?

- Ex. How long does Golfer have to decide whether to approve a proposed product? How long does ABC have to cure defects? How are payments determined in the interim?

13. Issues of Enforceability

- Be careful with clauses that may be deemed legally unenforceable, such as those that lack mutuality or provide for specific performance in "personal service contracts."

14. Don't Forget the Matter at Hand

- Remember to address key issues such as Player's "mandatory" participation in the Dubai Classic.

15. Include Schedule of Payments

- How/when will each party be paid? Can Golfer earn performance bonuses?
- Is late payment of owed monies grounds for termination?
- When does reimbursement of player's expenses occur?
- Do income streams pass on to heirs and assigns?

16. Boilerplate: Waiver, Severability, Governing Law, Entire Understanding

- A party's failure to exercise particular rights does not constitute waiver.
- If any provision of the agreement is found invalid, the rest of the agreement will not be affected.
- Which state's law governs?
- "The agreement reflects the entire understanding of the parties and supersedes all prior agreements, both written and oral."

17. "Right" vs. Duty to Pursue Infringers

- Consider parties' (differing) incentives to pursue infringers, as well as the potential free-rider problem.

18. Using Legal "Forms"

- Using "forms" as a checklist to ensure that you aren't missing any key terms can be helpful, but do not rely exclusively on forms, lest they "run away with you."
- Make sure that each clause you see in a form is applicable to the current document before using it.
- Know that some forms are, for example, "Player friendly" while some may be "sponsor friendly."

2. Litigating the Agreement: Alleged Breach of "Suitability" and Related Clauses

Now it is time to assume the (inevitable?) "contract breach" litigation "hypothetical."

For this litigation hypothetical, assume that Player from the previous hypothetical signed an agreement with ABC with the following terms:

- Force majeure—There is a force majeure clause that references "terrorist attacks (or threats thereof)" as being a basis for the contract not requiring Player to play in the Dubai Open.
- Suitability—There is a "suitability" clause that requires Player to play ABC's clubs in the Dubai Open if, "in his reasonable professional judgment, such Clubs are suitable for use in PGA and other worldwide-tour competitive play."

- Morals clause and termination rights—For purposes of ABC's "termination rights," the "morals clause" prevents Player from engaging in any acts that, if proven, would constitute a "felony" under U.S. law.

- Exclusivity—There is a clause that requires Player to (exclusively) use ABC's clubs "whenever Player is in public."

- Non-disparagement—There is a standard non-disparagement clause, preventing Player from "publicly disparaging or undermining" the products.

Litigation Hypothetical's "Assumed Facts"

Given the foregoing contract terms, please assume the following facts:

- Osama Bin–Laden has been reported to be in the Dubai area, prior to the Tournament. He is also rumored to be threatening to launch a terrorist attack, prior to or during the Open.

- Upon arrival in Dubai, Player does not want to play ABC's Clubs, because he is nervous about the possible terrorist attacks and has gone on a drinking binge in Dubai as a result thereof, which might implicate the "morals" clause of the Endorsement Agreement.

- While in Dubai, Player has been drinking and, during a practice round, engaged in several acts of public drunkenness that were observed by other Tour players and spectators. At the same time, he did not perform well with the Clubs, and therefore has now deemed them *not* to be "suitable for use" in the Open while still "under the influence" of his practice round drinking.

- After his practice round, as he sobers up, Player goes back to his hotel room at The Dubai Divot Motel near the tournament course and begins taking practice swings in his room with his old Hogan clubs, with the curtains partially open.

(*Query*: is this a violations of Player's obligations to use ABC's products "whenever in public"?)

- The Player has begun privately to question the suitability of ABC's products. In particular, during his practice round, he has told his caddy ("in confidence") that "these clubs might be all right for somebody else on the Tour, but they just don't feel right to me—despite all the 'tweaking,' they just don't feel like my old Hogans!"

(*Query*: is this a violation of Player's "non-disparagement clause"?)

"You make the call." In pre-litigation, make the best arguments on each side, respectively (in each Group) for Player and ABC whether Player must play the clubs in the first round of the

Dubai Open. Please use your "litigating voice," in so doing. Also make your best arguments about what damages Player owes and why.

In calculating possible damages, consider further whether such "out of bounds" behavior by Player voids the "limited liability" clause that would otherwise require Player simply to return the payment that ABC had previously made to him, under a standard "limitation of liability" clause to which both parties have agreed. In so doing, you can assume that the limitation of liability clause prohibits the recovery of consequential damages, except in the case of "intentional wrongdoing" or a "material breach."

Alternatively, as ABC's attorney, consider whether ABC can recover all of its "consequential damages" proximately caused by Player's decision not to play ABC's clubs including, inter alia, (1) all "campaign rollout" media and advertising expenses from January 1 through the Dubai Open; (2) lost (projected) sales, including the costs associated with the sale of ABC clubs that are returned due to Player's reneging on his product endorsement; (3) damages proximately caused by ABC's inability to sign another Player for the upcoming PGA Tour season; (4) damages re: "reputational harm," which might prevent ABC from signing up another PGA Tour Player and/or having to pay significantly more than it agreed to pay the first Player.

After negotiating a possible resolution, but assuming a total "breakdown" of the relationship due to Player's "breaches," please now draft the section headings for a hypothetical brief arguing either Player's or ABC's position. For guidance on drafting brief headings, see the following "In Focus: Drafting Brief Headings."

IN FOCUS: DRAFTING BRIEF HEADINGS

Most law students are probably more familiar with drafting briefs than contracts, given the curricula in American law schools. The following tips, however, review some of the basics of drafting the headings for legal briefs in the context of representing a professional athlete. As you have seen, showing your "back teeth," and effectively using your "litigating voice" are essential tools to use, as and when appropriate, to effectively represent your professional athlete-client.

Put Best ("Why I Win!") Argument First

In drafting Brief Headings, you must attempt to assess the order of your arguments on the assumption that the judge (or clerk) reading your headings may well stop reading your headings after the very first one!

Accordingly, you should always try to put your "best argument first," in as succinct and persuasive a heading as possible, without "going overboard" to the point where you are so dismissive of your opposition's most likely "best argument" that you lose your credibility with the Court.

In so doing, whenever possible, you should encapsulate your Heading's facts within the "highest/most authoritative" legal precedent available to support your arguments. In other words, you should get to the "highest legal ground" on which you can stand, whether it be the U.S. Constitution itself; a relevant federal or state statute; or a directly controlling "on point" case precedent from the highest appellate (or supreme) court available to you.

"Honesty is the best policy" here, however. As indicated above, if you "overbid your hand" in your first Brief Heading, you may well lose your audience. Be certain, therefore, that any relevant "supporting authority" cited in the first Brief Heading cannot be undercut or effectively distinguished by the opposition. Similarly, in reciting the relevant supporting "facts of record," be certain that there are no "ellipses" or "omissions of material fact" that the opposition can exploit to destroy your credibility with the Court.

Your first few "narrative" Brief paragraphs, after the first Headings, should next flow naturally from the "introduction," which the reader has (hopefully) accepted. You can then provide a more thorough explication of the initial argument, while putting more "flesh on the bones" of the Heading's legal/factual skeleton. In so doing, your general rule should be "no surprises," lest the reader detect a deviation from the Heading theme on which you have implicitly promised to deliver in your narrative.

As you end the narrative of the first Brief section, you can begin to summarize again, without insulting the reader, "why I win," if the reader accepts only your first argument. In so doing, however, you should also begin gently directing the reader to your next "best argument," lest the reader (prematurely) compares the opponent's first "best argument," and decides the case (perhaps against you!). At a minimum, the reader must be convinced that he must "read on" in fairness to your client.[43]

Put Next–Best ("Why I Win!") Argument Second

After anticipating your next "best argument" at the end of the first Brief section, you will need to transition as seamlessly as possible by drafting your second "why I win" Brief Heading.

In so doing, the same general drafting principles should apply as described above—get to your "highest ground" of legal/precedential authority, and tailor-make the ("fairly read") facts to fit

---

43. The judicious use of "stair step" subheadings can, in a longer brief, also help to bridge the potential "attention deficit gap" that might overtake the reader in a particularly long narrative section.

within that framework. Again, any perceived "contortion" of the facts or the law will count against you. So, too, would be an overly hyperbolic or otherwise exaggerated conclusion. Courts/clerks like to be "led to the water," but not "forced to drink" by Brief Headings/narratives that are overly self-righteous or self-assured. After all, if there were not "another side of the story," the case would not be in litigation to begin with!

Suggesting (irreversible) conclusions to the Court should be the target, leaving room for the Court to agree that you have hit the "bulls eye"—perhaps with (unanticipated) "arrows" that you did not even realize might be in your "quiver," but for the Court's citing of a case/legal authority that you might have missed.

As you tease out the narrative in support of your second Brief Heading, you can "assume a lot" and "incorporate by reference" much of the factual predicate of your preceding argument, to the extent it applies.

As to the legal predicates, eye-catching undeniably relevant "direct hits" should be imbedded in your narrative, as you attempt to guide the Court/clerk how to write an Opinion in your favor, without being pedantic or condescending. "String cites" are generally disfavored, unless accompanied by a short summary of the cited cases which <u>add to</u>, (<u>i.</u>e., do not simply "repeat") the prior cases' holdings.

If you take one "false/(unsupportable) step" at this point in your brief-writing exercise, it could be fatal re: losing credibility. Accordingly, it may be appropriate at this point to begin to distinguish your opponent's (anticipated) "best case." In fact, you may even want to "concede" an opponent's best non-controlling counter-argument, if only to show that the Court's accepting it would still be consistent with an ultimate ruling in your favor. This even-handedness will lend further credibility to the (favorable) conclusion which you trust the Court will ultimately arrive at on its own.

Put Best ("Why I Don't Lose") Counter–Argument Last

In concluding your Brief, you must "give the devil his due," and admit that the opposition's "best arguments" are worthy of consideration but, ultimately, should be rejected when contrasted with yours.

Accordingly, your Brief Heading here will often take the form of "even if you believe (some point of) my opponent's argument," you should <u>not</u> rule in his favor, for the following reasons.

Here, you will need to tread very carefully in "enemy territory," while conceding as few non-conclusive opponents' points as possible. In so doing, fresh legal and factual precedents may need to be invoked, again with as "neutral" an interposition that leads the Court to its own ineluctible conclusion that the opponent's "best argument" is, at the end of the briefing cycle, unavailing.

In certain "clear loser cases," however, this final part of the Brief may also have to do significant "damage control," by minimizing the opponent's recovery, should he win. Equitable/"unclean hands" types of arguments and/or "unjust enrichment" claims may be necessary, to avoid a catastrophic loss, as you throw yourself on the mercy of the Court to "personalize" your client to avoid a "punitive damages" award.

Conclusion

In closing, of course, in every type of case, you will return to your "why I must win—(and win big!)" mantra, harvesting the "seeds of victory" that you have been sowing throughout your Brief. As you do so, it can be helpful to "remind" the Court, in a non-threatening way, that ruling in your client's favor would simply be the (non-reversible) "right thing to do."

As a potential "iron fist" within that "velvet glove," though, you may also want to alert the Court (as an "officer" of same!), to the "reversibility consequences" that the Court would suffer if the Court flew in the face of your Brief's irrefutable logic and somehow ruled in favor of your opponent.[44]

Finally, be very clear in your conclusion re: what relief you are seeking so as to "monetize" same for the Court. In effect, without being presumptuous, you can conclude with the equivalent of a "draft Order" which the Court/clerk can adopt if you have won the case.

Pre–Filing/Post–Brief Writing "Tips"

After finalizing your Brief, if time permits, you should put it aside, and not review/revise it again for a pre-determined period of time. Then, before filing it, you should make sure that you have not "fallen in love with your own brief" because you got too close to it during the drafting process.

In so doing, you could, inter alia, read aloud your Brief Headings to a colleague familiar with the case, in a simulated "oral argument" environment. You can then call upon the colleague to make the best counter-argument for the opposition. By working your way through the Brief Headings in seriatim fashion, you can

---

44. These Brief Heading/Brief Writing "pointers" are meant to be used in the context of Hypothetical litigation-related exercises created for use in Professor Peter Carfagna's "Sports and the Law" classes. They do not reflect the opinions of any third-party, and do not depend upon the facts of any currently pending matters on which the author has previously worked, or may currently be working.

ensure the optimal structure/ordering of your Brief Headings, and fine tune any perceived weaknesses in them. You can also begin to decide which of your weakest arguments could be conceded, if/when the opposition exploits them either at oral argument or in a responsive brief.

Finally, then, by testing your arguments against a "devil's advocate" colleague in this way, you can feel most confident that the essence of the Brief's best argument should withstand the most carefully crafted "frontal attacks" by the opposition.

Chapter 4

PUBLICITY RIGHTS AND THE PROFESSIONAL ATHLETE

The first three chapters of this book introduced the basics about representing the professional athlete. They explained the scope of the relationship between the player and the agent and the laws and regulations that govern the relationship. They also provided a brief introduction to negotiation, legal drafting and litigating in this area. In this chapter, the focus now turns towards the substantive law that agents will encounter while representing professional athletes. In particular, it focuses on the "publicity rights" and other intellectual property rights which the professional athlete must exploit.

In today's lucrative sports marketing industry, professional athletes are constantly used to advertise products. Whether through endorsements, merchandising, or sponsorships, superstar athletes are increasingly leveraging their athletic accomplishments on the field into profitable contracts off the field by promoting commercial products. In the cases of the highest-paid athletes, many earn more money from endorsements and other commercial activities than from salary and winnings.[45]

To protect the commercial value of their identities, athletes rely on the "right of publicity." The right of publicity is now commonly recognized as a form of protection against the misappropriation of an individual's identity for commercial purposes. Yet, the legal landscape of the right of publicity still remains rather uncertain. Questions like what exactly constitutes "identity" and what types of uses are considered "commercial" continue to plague the courts. Even more difficult questions arise when courts are

45. The list includes golfer Tiger Woods, basketball players Shaquille O'Neal and LeBron James, baseball players Derek Jeter and Alex Rodriguez, football quarterback Peyton Manning, and soccer player David Beckham.

forced to balance an athlete's publicity rights with another's First Amendment rights to "artistic" freedom of expression. In those cases, the courts must determine whether on the one hand, the product being sold predominantly exploits the athlete's identity, or on the other hand, the product carries enough expressive content to warrant First Amendment protection.

The following chapter will provide an overview of the right of publicity. Beginning with a history of the development of the right of publicity, the chapter will go on to address the licensing of athletes' identities as well as strategies to use when drafting a licensing agreement. The next two sections will then outline how to argue right of publicity infringement claims and the most common defenses. The chapter will conclude with a look at the future of publicity rights.

A.   *History of Publicity Rights*

The "right of publicity" recognizes an individual's interest in controlling the commercial use of his or her identity and thus allows athletes to profit financially from the use of their name or likeness in products and services. Because intellectual property rights restrict free expression, the right of publicity and the First Amendment co-exist in tension. Consequently, some commercial uses of an athlete's identity may be deemed free expression rather than publicity rights infringement. The law and the courts determine where to draw the line between them. The right of publicity is a state law doctrine that grew out of the "right to privacy" first articulated by Samuel Warren and Louis Brandeis in 1890.[46] Several decades later, William Prosser identified four distinct invasion of privacy torts: (1) intrusion upon physical solitude; (2) public disclosure of private facts; (3) depiction in a false light in the public eye; and (4) appropriation of name or likeness.[47] Early cases dealt with a right to privacy allowing people to "block the use of their names and likenesses in advertisements without their consent."[48]

However, for celebrities, including famous athletes, there was significant doubt over whether the right to privacy applied, since they had voluntarily made themselves public figures. In *O'Brien v. Pabst Sales*,[49] former All–American quarterback Davey O'Brien sued Pabst over the beer company's use of his image next to a

46. Samuel Warren and Louis Brandeis, *The Right to Privacy*, 4 HARV. L. REV. 193 (1890).

47. William Prosser, *Privacy*, 48 CAL. L. REV. 383, 389 (1960).

48. See *Pavesich v. New England Life Insurance*, 122 Ga. 190, 50 S.E. 68 (1905). Courts in New York, however, reached a contrary result in *Roberson v.* *Rochester Folding Box*, 171 N.Y. 538, 64 N.E. 442 (1902), prompting the New York legislature to pass §§ 50 and 51 of the Civil Rights Law, making it actionable to use the "name, portrait or picture of any living person ... for advertising purposes, or for the purposes of trade ... without having first obtained the written consent of such person."

49. 124 F.2d 167 (5th Cir. 1941).

picture of a glass of beer on its annual football calendar. The court dismissed the case on the grounds that O'Brien had no reasonable expectation of privacy anymore and the calendar's use of his image did not contain or constitute his explicit endorsement of Pabst. For many years, the greatest athletes, including Joe DiMaggio, Joe Louis, and Babe Ruth, enjoyed no right of publicity during their careers.[50]

That changed with *Haelan Laboratories, Inc. v. Topps Chewing Gum, Inc.*,[51] when the court recognized for the first time, based on state common law, an assignable right to the "publicity value of one's name and picture."[52] The court refused to allow Topps to sell baseball cards with players' photos when those players had granted an exclusive license for this type of use to a competitor of Topps.

> [I]t is common knowledge that many prominent persons (especially actors and ball-players), far from having their feelings bruised through public exposure of their likenesses, would feel sorely deprived if they no longer received money for authorizing advertisements, popularizing their countenances, displayed in newspapers, magazines, buses, trains and subways. This right of publicity would usually yield them no money unless it could be made the subject of an exclusive grant which barred any other advertiser from using their pictures.[53]

In essence, the court recognized that the fourth tort identified by Prosser was different than the other three in that it protected important property or economic rights.[54] This is also emphasized by The Restatement (Third) of Unfair Competition, which defines an infringer of the right of publicity as "[o]ne who appropriates the commercial value of a person's identity by using without consent the person's name, likeness, or other indicia of identity for purposes of trade."[55]

In *Zacchini v. Scripps–Howard Broadcasting*,[56] the only time the right was considered by Supreme Court, the court held that a performer had a right of publicity in his "human cannonball" show,

50. Paul Weiler & Gary Roberts, Sports and the Law 473 (3d ed. 2004).

51. 202 F.2d 866, 868 (2d Cir. 1953).

52. *Id.*

53. *Id.*

54. Weiler & Roberts, *supra* note 50, at 473. In fact, however, in *Pirone v. MacMillan*, 894 F.2d 579 (2d Cir. 1990), the court acknowledged that Haelan no longer held sway in New York, as there existed no common law rights to privacy or publicity apart from the statutory rights.

55. The Restatement (Third) of Unfair Competition § 46 (1995). "The name, likeness, and other indicia of a person's identity are used 'for purposes of trade' under the rule stated in § 46 if they are used in advertising the user's goods or services, or are placed on merchandise marketed by the user, or are used in connection with services rendered by the user. However, use 'for purposes of trade' does not ordinarily include the use of a person's identity in news reporting, commentary, entertainment, works of fiction or nonfiction, or in advertising that is incidental to such uses." *Id.* at § 47.

56. 433 U.S. 562 (1977).

and that this right was violated by a news report broadcasting the entire show (which took fifteen seconds).[57] The Court, building upon the ideas of Prosser noted above, describes the purpose of the right of publicity as "closely analogous to the goals of patent and copyright law, focusing on the right of the individual to reap the reward of his endeavors and having little to do with protecting feelings or reputation."[58] Perhaps the most difficult, and novel, passage in *Zacchini* is the following: "Moreover, the broadcast of petitioner's entire performance, unlike the unauthorized use of another's name for purposes of trade or the incidental use of a name or picture by the press, goes to the heart of petitioner's ability to earn a living as an entertainer."[59] Although it does not do so explicitly, it appears the Court is injecting a balancing test, such that the right of publicity is stronger when the appropriation "goes to the heart of" a person's ability to make a living. Presumably, therefore, the right of publicity is weaker when the appropriation does not adversely affect a person's economic interests.

Later cases place increased emphasis on whether the celebrity or athlete's identity was "commercially exploited." For example, in *Carson v. Here's Johnny Portable Toilets, Inc.*,[60] the Court held that the use of the phrases "Here's Johnny" and "The World's Foremost Commodian" violated the real comic's right of publicity, even though his name was not used, because it was clear that the public would identify those phrases with his identity.[61] Similarly, in *Ali v. Playgirl, Inc.*,[62] the court held that a drawing of a man in a boxing ring with the phrase "The Greatest" was sufficient to violate Muhammad Ali's right of publicity.[63] Indeed, another court held that the use of the name "Crazylegs" for a women's shaving cream violated famous football player Elroy Hirsch's right of publicity because "Crazylegs" was his nickname.[64] Yet another case, *Doe v. TCI Cablevision*,[65] found that hockey player Tony Twist's right of publicity was violated by a cartoon's use of his name for one of its characters.[66]

Hoping for further Supreme Court enlightenment and guidance, the lower courts have used a patchwork of tests and policies to examine matters on a case-by-case basis to protect both the freedom of expression and each celebrity's cultivated identity.

---

57. *Id.* at 563–64. Specifically, the Court rejected the contention that the First and Fourteenth Amendments trumped the right of publicity in this case. *Id.* at 564.

58. *Id.* at 573.

59. *Id.* at 576.

60. 698 F.2d 831 (6th Cir. 1983).

61. *Id.* at 833–34.

62. 447 F. Supp 723 (S.D.N.Y. 1978).

63. *Id.* at 726–27.

64. *See* Hirsch v. S.C. Johnson & Son, Inc., 280 N.W.2d 129 (Wis. 1979).

65. 110 S.W.3d 363 (Mo. 2003).

66. *Id.* at 370.

The relative dearth of case law regarding publicity rights and the varied interpretations and statutes across jurisdictions mean that one cannot with utmost clarity articulate the current state of the law in this field. Skilled practitioners can, however, prepare themselves to best safeguard their clients' interests through private law by recognizing and optimizing the elements of a deal most relevant to rights to publicity.

IN FOCUS: NEGOTIATING AND DRAFTING A LICENSE AGREEMENT

In light of the inconsistent application of player publicity rights in the courts, as well as the lucrative nature of using players' names and likenesses, many companies and advertisers negotiate licenses to make use of a player's identity in connection with their product. While the state law right to publicity will generally serve as the legal background to these negotiations, the parties have significant latitude to craft their licensing agreements in a manner that both sides find beneficial. As a result, attorneys for celebrity athletes must be careful to delineate exactly what aspects of the player's identity are being licensed and under what terms those particular aspects are to be used. The following pages will provide a close examination of key clauses in a standard licensing agreement and offer suggestions about how to draft each section to maximize protection for the athlete.

Definitions

License agreements should begin with a list of definitions of the key terms to be used in the agreement. The definitions should eliminate any ambiguity and provide a clear and concise understanding of the relevant term. Attorneys should avoid overly broad or narrow definitions that may create confusion and increase the chance of litigation.

Attorneys should generally refrain from using any terms that are undefined or ambiguous, and when defined terms are used, they should be capitalized to accord them their intended meaning. Lastly, attorneys must be cautious when using legal terms of art that are common-day synonyms but carry different meaning in the context of a licensing agreement, i.e. "terminate" and "void," which have separate and distinct legal meanings.

Grant/Reservation of Rights

Every license agreement should include a section defining the scope of the license. It should detail what rights are being granted to the licensee and what rights are being reserved to the licensor. Specifically, the section should identify if the player's name, likeness, voice, performance, signature or any other identifying feature, or combination thereof, are being granted. The section should also expressly state that all features of his identity not granted are expressly reserved.

This section should also define the types of media or forums in which the player's identity can be used. Whether the license includes print, television, radio, or internet uses should be clearly set out in the language of the agreement. The host of newly developed uses for player identities now available on the internet via fantasy leagues, video games, streaming video and beyond has made this section increasingly important. As such, licensees must be sure to reserve the right to exploit their rights of publicity in any media including all forms of media now known or hereafter devised.

In addition, the section should include the duration of the agreement, whether the rights granted are transferable or assignable, and address any other future contingencies such as potential extensions or expansions of the licensing agreement.

Restrictions on Use

Oftentimes players will want to retain a certain amount of oversight or quality control with regards to the use of their identity. The question of how much oversight a player retains will often depend on the caliber of both the player and the sponsering company, as well as the particular relationship between the two parties. In the more restrictive agreements, players will require that they give explicit approval before the use can be marketed. These agreements should outline whether written approval is required, whether approval cannot be unreasonably withheld, and should also set out a timetable for the player to review the use and for the licensee to cure any potential defects.

Exclusivity

The agreement should also state whether the license is exclusive. Most companies will seek exclusive provisions to secure the value of their investment. Specifically, a company will require that no licenses are granted to any of the company's competitors. While such arrangements are common in license agreements, the attorney for the celebrity athlete should be sure to incorporate specific language defining "competitors" of the licensee company. Additionally, if a player desires any exceptions to this exclusivity for charitable purposes or otherwise, they should be explicitly stated in the agreement.

Termination

License agreements can create litigation for a variety of reasons. The termination clause should outline exactly what consequences will ensue upon a breach of the contract. It should indicate which clauses, if violated, would result in a material breach. It should also indicate what types of breach, if any, require notice and an opportunity to cure before the agreement can be terminated.

Remedies/Post–Termination Rights

In addition to termination provisions, the license agreement should also explain what remedies or damages are available for the different types of breaches. This section should include what type of damages are available (consequential, punitive, etc.), how they are calculated, and whether there is a limitation of liability. It should also indicate whether separate remedies are available for different classes of breaches.

The section should also spell out post-termination rights, namely who retains ownership of unsold merchandise or works in production and whether the existing revenue stream will continue.

Other Provisions

Schedules of Payment

- How and when will each party be paid?
- Are there performance bonuses for the player?
- Do late payments constitute a ground for termination?
- Do income streams pass on to heirs and assigns?

Choice of Law

- Which state law governs?
- Does that state strongly recognize the right to publicity? (The protection afforded by individual states can vary).

Boilerplate Language

- Waiver: A party's failure to exercise particular rights does not constitute waiver.
- Severability: If any provision of the agreement is found invalid, the rest of the agreement will not be affected.
- Entire Understanding: The agreement reflects the entire understanding of the parties and supersedes all prior agreements, both written and oral.

Right vs. Duty to Pursue Infringers

- Do either of the parties have a duty to pursue infringers?
- Does the arrangement benefit either of the parties, or create a potential free-rider problem?

General Considerations

Internal Consistency/ References

- The agreement should maintain consistency throughout. Use of defined terms and citations referring back to particular clauses can ensure internal consistency.

Enforceability

- While an attorney must seek to negotiate the best possible agreement for his client, he must also be careful not to include clauses that will be deemed legally unenforceable, i.e. clauses lacking mutuality or requiring specific performance.

Using Forms

- As previously noted, attorneys often use previous forms when creating license agreements. Forms can be effective as checklists, but an attorney should make sure that each clause in the form is applicable to the current agreement before using it. Finally, an attorney must be aware that some forms are "licensor friendly" while others are "licensee friendly."

Chapter 4, Section A—Questions for Discussion

Now it is time to apply all of these drafting "tips" to the following "hypothetical" License Agreement. ("Exemplar" responses are, as usual, set forth in the Teacher's Manual.)

Negotiating a License Agreement: The Hypothetical

Assume the following facts for purposes of negotiating and drafting a "license agreement" for the creation of a proposed lithograph poster for a PGA Tour Player who has just won his first "Major."

1. PGA Tour Player ("Player" or "Golfer") has been on the Tour for two years and has achieved unparalleled success. He has just won his first "Major," but so far only has exploited the "product endorsement" category with respect to certain of his clubs (i.e., his irons, only, but not his putter or his woods). His other "endorsement categories" thus remain "saleable," including his "publicity rights," as they relate to a "lithograph poster" category. Also, his "autograph" category remains untapped with respect to any endorsement category, including golf clubs or posters.

2. Player has been approached by a second-rate lithograph poster artist Freddie Flair ("Artist"), who has created a photograph-like rendering of Player winning his first Major, on the 18th green. Artist claims that he has "captured" Player's "signature fist pump" as the winning putt drops in the hole. He also has surrounded the "fist pump" depiction with a collage of other photograph-like depictions including: Player's "signature swing finish" on his last shot into the 18th green, and Player's

embracing his parents on the 18th green after winning the Major.

3. Artist claims that his proposed lithograph poster is "creative expression," which he is entitled to sell, whether or not he has Player's permission to do so. Nonetheless, Artist wants to seek Player's authorization to sell the proposed poster as the only "officially Player-licensed" poster "commemorating" Player's winning his first Major. Artist also wants to create a "limited edition" of the poster, which Player would autograph, so that Artist can sell same at a higher price-point.

4. Artist claims that his unique "artistic contribution" to the poster product is as follows: he obtains the rights to the relevant photographs of Golfer and then digitally reproduces them on the first draft of the collage on the poster by connecting them in time-ordered sequence. In the case of this poster, he then digitally "connected" the three photos in a "uniquely creative" way, which he calls his "distinctive flair." He then poetically themes the poster with a uniquely creative title. In this case, he has titled his digital reproduction "The Home Hole."

5. Player's attorney/agent has "auctioned" this category by seeking an offer to create a similar poster from other more famous sports artists (including Leroy Neiman), but Artist's offer is more than double what any other artist will offer. Player tells his agent/attorney that he wants Artist to "show him the money," and, if the deal is rich enough, with enough opt-out quality control and other "protections" built in, Player would consider entering into a license agreement with Artist. In so doing, however, Player wants to preserve his "rights of publicity" and autograph-related rights for future exploitation in other categories, including his eventual "signature line" of golf clubs.

In light of these facts, consider the previous section "In Focus: Negotiating and Drafting a Licensing Agreement" as well as the "exemplars" contained in the Teacher's Manual.

Break up into your sub-Groups, with each sub-Group assigned to represent either Golfer or Artist in a pre-negotiation strategy session. (If your sub-Group represented the Player last time, it should represent the Artist this time and vice versa.)

In your sub-Group strategy session, consider the following negotiating strategies and prepare appropriate drafting strategies to prepare for a "do or die" negotiation session with the other side:

a. "Definitions" section, to encompass "licensed products" and to exclude (or not) any trademark or other intellectual property rights Golfer might otherwise claim to own.

b. "Grant of rights" by Golfer, and limitation (or expansion) of same. "Reservation of rights" by Golfer for any other non-granted rights, including reference to autograph rights (or not).

c. "Rights of approval" for Golfer over Artist's "creative expression" (or not), including the need to obtain such approval "in writing" (or not).

d. Costs allocation, in the event of Golfer's refusing to approve a proposed poster that Artist believes is of satisfactory quality for publication and sale.

e. "Ownership rights" over the "original creation," and an acknowledgement (or not) by Golfer that the "original" does not infringe on any of Golfer's "rights of publicity."

f. A damages/remedies clause, including a "limitation of liability clause" (or not), as well as the right to injunctive relief or specific performance if/when either party deems it necessary/appropriate.

g. A dispute resolution and "confidentiality" clause, if the parties' respective leverage/self-interest dictates the drafting of same.

h. A "renegotiation clause," if Golfer's career continues to take off, and more famous artists become willing to create a higher quality lithograph poster for Golfer.

i. A "termination clause" if Artist floods the market with a greater number of posters than the agreement permits.

j. A "right to pursue infringers" clause, to initiate litigation if/when "knock off" artists try to sell counterfeit renderings that are "confusingly similar" to Artist's poster.

As you prepare to enter the negotiation session with your sub-Group's strategies, list your ZOPAs, NOPAs, and BATNAs (if any), and the reasons therefore. Also list your "must haves," "throwaways," and "leverage points," based on the fact pattern and your understanding of the relevant case law (i.e., ETW vs. Jireh, considered later in this chapter, and the cases cited therein.)

Consider which "negotiating voice" you will use, and why, given the foregoing. Also consider what "pre-litigation" threats you will use, if any, and when/why.

Prepare to advise your client re: the likely litigation outcome, if Artist proceeds to sell the lithograph poster without Golfer's permission, and Golfer sues to enjoin such sales. Factor such advice into your negotiating strategy, to determine your ultimate strategy and "leverage points," etc., as your "negotiation" leads to the "drafting" of a "litigation proof" agreement.

Please see the Teacher's Manual for creative "exemplar" resolutions of this "hypothetical."

B. Constructing a Right of Publicity Infringement Claim

As we have seen, publicity rights are protected by both state and federal laws. Under state law, the degree of protection varies from state to state. Many states have enacted explicit statutes recognizing publicity rights. Other states recognize a common-law right of publicity. Some states recognize both. Some states recognize neither. As a result, plaintiffs and defendants are well-served by understanding the specific protection afforded by their state and how it differs from other jurisdictions.

In addition to state claims, plaintiffs may also allege a violation of their publicity rights under § 43(a) of the federal Lanham Act. The Lanham Act provides protection against the use of false designations of origin, false descriptions, and false representations in the advertising and sale of goods and services. The elements of each of these claims are discussed in more detail below.

Right of Publicity Infringement Claims Under State Law

As noted above, state laws do not provide uniform protection. However, most state laws generally name three key elements to a right of publicity claim: (1) that defendant used plaintiff's identity (2) without consent (3) for commercial purposes.

Identity

The first thing a plaintiff must demonstrate in a successful right of publicity claim is that the defendant made use of the plaintiff's identity. The identity inquiry is a question of fact depending upon the nature and extent of the identifying characteristics used by the defendant, the defendant's intent, the fame of the plaintiff, evidence of actual identification made by third persons, and surveys or other evidence indicating the perceptions of the audience.[67] Courts have explained that the central issue is whether consumers will connect the plaintiff with the defendant's use in the advertisement.

For example, in *Carson v. Here's Johnny Portable Toilets, Inc.*, the issue was whether the defendant's use of the phrases "Here's Johnny" and "The World's Foremost Commodian" to sell portable toilets was a violation of Carson's publicity rights.[68] There, the identity inquiry was simply whether consumers would connect this

---

67. Restatement 3d of Unfair Competition, § 46.

68. *Carson v. Here's Johnny Portable Toilets, Inc.*, 698 F.2d 831, 835 (6th Cir. 1983).

advertisement to Carson. In *TCI*, the question was whether consumers would connect the comic book character "Anthony 'Tony Twist' Twistelli" to the actual hockey player Tony Twist who shared similar qualities to the comic book character.[69] In *Ali*, the issue was whether consumers would connect champion boxer Muhammad Ali to a picture of a black man sitting on a stool in the corner of a ring with the caption "The Greatest."[70] In all of these cases, the courts found that the advertisements sufficiently made use of the plaintiff's identity such that consumers would connect the plaintiff to the defendant's use.

Other cases involving the identity element include:

- A company hires a "sound-alike" of Bette Midler to perform popular songs for a series of commercials advertising automobiles. The commercials did not make use of Midler's name or face, and the company had a license to use the song from the copyright holder. The court found such imitation to violate Midler's right of publicity in her voice. *Midler v. Ford Motor Co.*, 849 F.2d 460 (9th Cir. 1988). In its holding, the court distinguished previous cases denying protection to "sound-alikes" stating that those plaintiff's sought protection in the performance of the song rather than the distinctive nature of the voice itself. See c.f. *Sinatra v. Goodyear Tire & Rubber Co.*, 435 F.2d 711 (9th Cir.1970), cert. denied 402 U.S. 906, 91 S.Ct. 1376, 28 L.Ed.2d 646 (1971)

- A woman's shaving gel company decided to advertise its product by making use of a famous athlete's nickname, "Crazylegs." While the company admitted the use was without consent, they argued the use was not exclusively in reference to the athlete. The court held that the allegation of unauthorized use was sufficient to state a cause of action. *Hirsch v. S.C. Johnson & Son, Inc.*, 90 Wis.2d 379, 280 N.W.2d 129 (1979). Compare this result to a different case involving a woodcarver who sued Columbia Pictures for the unauthorized use of his name, "T.J. Hooker," in their new police drama. The court observed that the decision to name the leading police detective "T.J. Hooker" was not intended to identify the plaintiff, and his specialized craft of carving wooden ducks. The court furthermore held that where the use of a plaintiff's name does not sufficiently identify the plaintiff, there can be no relief. *Hooker v. Columbia Pictures Industries, Inc.*, 551 F.Supp. 1060 (N.D.Ill.1982)

- To promote an electrical company, an advertising agency created a robot that dressed and posed like Vanna White

---

69. *TCI*, 110 S.W.3d at 369–70.   **70.** *Ali*, 447 F. Supp. at 728.

next to a "Wheel of Fortune" set. The court held such use sufficiently identified her to state a cause of action under California common law, but not statutory law.

- A tobacco company used a famous driver's car to advertise its products. While the district court held that the plaintiff was not identified visually, orally, explicitly, or inferentially, the Ninth Circuit overturned holding that the distinctive features of the car were peculiar to the defendant and implicated his identity. *Motschenbacher v. R.J. Reynolds Tobacco Co.*, 498 F.2d 821 (9th Cir. 1974)

In general, these cases point to a more flexible understanding of identity to accommodate for the realities of marketing. Companies that make use of celebrities' identities are usually doing so to increase the attention brought to their product. If consumers are unable to identify the celebrity in the advertisement, then the purpose of the advertisement is largely lost. While cases involving race cars or imitation robots may pose some difficulty, the more standard usage of names and likenesses will almost always satisfy the identity standard.

Consent

The second element a plaintiff must prove is lack of consent. No person may exploit the commercial value of an individual's identity without the consent of the individual, the assignee or the license holder to use the name or likeness.

Consent can be granted in a number of ways. The consent may be expressly declared in formal agreements like licenses or assignments. Or if the particular state statute does not require that consent be in writing, consent can also be implied from conduct that can be reasonably understood as manifesting consent. Importantly, consent in the form of a license or agreement does not transfer ownership to the licensee, but rather sets out the conditions upon which the licensee may exploit the licensor's identity. Note however that in most cases, lack of consent is not difficult to establish and is rarely litigated.

Commercial Purposes

The third element a plaintiff must establish is that his or her identity was used for commercial purposes. In general, use of the plaintiff's identity in an advertisement or promotion for a particular product will satisfy this requirement. The advertisement need not imply that the plaintiff endorses the product, nor does it have to be false, deceptive or misleading to establish that it was used for a commercial purpose. On the contrary, courts have broadly interpreted commercial purposes to mean any use of a plaintiff's identity that attracts consumers to the defendant's product.

For example, in *Abdul–Jabbar v. Gen. Motors*, defendants used Kareem Abdul Jabbar's birth name, Lewis Alcindor, to advertise their product. There the court held that "to the extent GMC's use of the plaintiff's birth name attracted television's viewers attention, GMC gained a commercial advantage."[71] Similarly, in *Eastwood v. Superior Court for Los Angeles County*, a tabloid newspaper published a false story about a love triangle involving famous actor Clint Eastwood. Noting the exploitation of Eastwood's name, photograph and likeness, the court held the use to constitute a commercial purpose explaining that "the first step toward selling a product or service is to attract the consumers' attention."[72]

However, not all uses of a plaintiff's identity are commercial. Uses such as news reporting, editorials, parodies, biographies and even fictionalized stories of real people's lives have all been found to be non-commercial. In such instances, courts will often balance the commercial nature of the advertisement with the expressive content and its resulting First Amendment protection. For example, in *Hoffman v. Capitol Cities/ABC, Inc.*, a magazine digitally altered a picture of Dustin Hoffman from a role he played in the motion picture, Tootsie.[73] Despite making use of his identity, the court found that the use combined fashion photography, humor and expressive content. As such, the court held that such usage was not a traditional advertisement designed solely for commercial purposes.

Increasingly, scholars and courts alike are promoting a spectrum-based version of the commercial purposes analysis. On the highly commercial end are uses that imply association or endorsement between the plaintiff and the defendant's product. These uses will almost certainly establish the commercial purposes element. On the non-commercial end are expressive uses that are not merely for commercial gain. These types of uses will require the court to balance the commercial versus expressive nature of the advertisement. Ultimately, where a particular use falls along this spectrum will depend on the particular facts and context of each case.

Policy Considerations

In addition to the statutory requirements, courts also consider five general policy justifications for upholding a player's publicity rights: (1) protection of an individual's interest in dignity and autonomy; (2) securing for plaintiffs the commercial value of their fame; (3) preventing unjust enrichment of others seeking to appro-

---

71. *Abdul–Jabbar v. General Motors*, 85 F.3d 407, 415–16 (9th Cir. 1996).

72. *Eastwood v. Superior Court of Los Angeles County*, 149 Cal. App.3d 409 (1983).

73. *Hoffman v. Capital Cities/ABC, Inc.*, 255 F.3d 1180 (9th Cir. 2001).

priate the commercial value of plaintiff's fame for themselves; (4) preventing harmful or excessive use that may dilute the value of one's identity; and (5) affording protection against false suggestions or endorsement of sponsorship.[74]

(1) Protection of an individual's interest in dignity and autonomy

The first prong recognizes the players' interests in dignity and autonomy. Both of these elements relate to a more fundamental aspect of publicity rights: control. Courts have consistently recognized that publicity rights are ultimately about players' ability to control the commercialization of their names. For example, in *TCI*, the court stated that "the right of publicity is the inherent right of every human being to control the commercial use of his or her identity."[75]

(2) Securing for plaintiffs the commercial value of their fame

The second policy reason for the right of publicity is the need to protect one's right to secure the commercial value of his fame. In today's sports marketing world of video games, playing cards, interactive web games, jersey sales, collector items, magazines, commercials and a host of other financial opportunities, players' names and likenesses have become considerably profitable. With this background in mind, many courts recognize the need to protect players' rights to capitalize on their fame.

However, many courts are hesitant to recognize this prong as a valid basis for upholding publicity rights. These courts rely on the *Zacchini* case where the Supreme Court found that the broadcast of the performer's entire performance would "go to the heart" of his ability to earn a living as an entertainer. While publicity rights are profitable, they do not go to the "heart" of players' earnings because they are already receiving sizeable salaries. The reasoning follows that since players already make enough money, they will still have an economic incentive to work hard and develop their talent.

(3) Preventing unjust enrichment of others seeking to appropriate the commercial value of plaintiff's fame for themselves

The third policy consideration relates to the prevention of unjust enrichment on the part of the defendant. The best common counter-argument posed by defendants is that there is no unjust enrichment because the names

74. Restatement (Third) of Unfair Competition Section 46, Cmt. C (2005).

75. *TCI*, 110 S.W.3d at 368.

and likenesses of famous athletes are readily available in the public domain. However, plaintiffs are quick to respond that player names and likenesses have value exactly because they are in the public domain.

For example in *Uhlaender v. Henricksen,* 316 F. Supp. 1277 (U.S.D.C. Minn. 1970), the defendant company created a sports game using players' names and statistics without players' permission. There, the court specifically rejected this public domain argument, noting that "[p]layer names and statistics are valuable only because of their past public disclosure, publicity and circulation. . . . To hold that such publicity destroys a right to sue for appropriation of a name or likeness would negate any and all causes of action, for only disclosure and public acceptance does the name of a celebrity have any value at all to make its unauthorized use enjoinable."[76]

(4) Preventing harmful or excessive use that may dilute the value of one's identity

The fourth prong relates to the need to protect players from uses that will dilute the value of their identity. This prong can be especially difficult for plaintiffs when the allegedly infringing use appears to improve the commercial value of the player's identity. For example, in *C.B.C. Distrib. & Mktg. v. Major League Baseball Advanced, L.P.*, 505 F.3d 818, (8th Cir. Mo. 2007), the defendant fantasy company persuasively argued that fantasy sports leagues actually enhance the marketability of players.

In response, plaintiffs should be quick to point out that such business decisions are best left to individual parties who are much more capable of understanding the intricacies of sports marketing than the court. Plaintiffs should further emphasize that many players seek to create a particular image in order to enhance their reputation and boost endorsement opportunities. They choose what trading cards they sign, what commercials they are in, what products they endorse, what video games they are featured in, and a host of other marketing decisions. As a result, they should also control how their names and likenesses are used in public.

(5) Affording protection against false suggestions of endorsement or sponsorship

The fifth and final prong protects players from companies that falsely suggest or imply that a player endorses

76. *Uhlaender*, 316 F.Supp. at 1282–83.

their product. Player endorsements have become a sizeable source of revenue for many athletes, especially the superstars of their respective sport. For example, in October of 2007 Gatorade announced that Tiger Woods will have his own brand of sports drink called "Gatorade Tiger" that will pay him $100 million over five years. In 2003 (before he even entered the NBA), Lebron James signed a seven-year shoe deal with Nike worth more than $90 million.

To protect these valuable contracts, plaintiffs must emphasize the highly commercial nature of using a player's name to promote a particular product. The contracts of Woods and James are prime examples of the commercial value of such endorsements. Plaintiffs can further argue that unlike other uses that may qualify as protected expression, endorsements and sponsorships are primarily—if not completely—designed to attract consumer's attention to the company's product.

Having established the basic elements and policy arguments for right of publicity infringement claims under state law, the next section will describe the claims brought under federal law.

Right of Publicity Under Federal Law

Celebrity athletes can also bring federal law claims under Section 43(a) of the Lanham Act, 15 U.S.C. § 1125(a), which prohibits the use of false descriptions of origin, false descriptions, and false representations in the advertising and sale of goods and services. In the context of sports marketing, courts have recognized false endorsement claims under Section 43(a) of the Lanham Act where a celebrity athlete's image or identity is used in connection with a product in such a way that implies the athlete endorses the product. Although the Lanham Act primarily deals with trademarks, courts have explained that when a false endorsement claim is brought under Section 43(a), the "mark" at issue is the plaintiff's identity. As one court explained, "A false endorsement claim based on the unauthorized use of a celebrity's identity is a type of false association claim, for it alleges the misuse of a trademark, *i.e.*, a symbol or device such as a visual likeness, vocal imitation, or other uniquely distinguishing characteristic, which is likely to confuse consumers as to the plaintiff's sponsorship or approval of the product."[77]

In the standard false endorsement claim, the controlling issue is the likelihood of confusion that consumers will believe the celebrity athlete has endorsed the product. Courts have developed eight factors to determine if such a likelihood of confusion exists:

key to false endorsement claim is confusion of consumers

8 factors

77. Waits v. Frito–Lay, Inc., 978 F.2d 1093 (9th Cir. 1992).

(1) Strength of plaintiff's mark—If a plaintiff has a very strong, recognizable mark in the sense that the consuming public connects the plaintiff's mark or identity to plaintiff's goods, it is more likely that consumers will be confused about the source or endorsement of the defendant's products.

(2) Relatedness of goods—Where the defendant and plaintiff make use of the plaintiff's mark or identity in similar ways, there is a higher likelihood that consumers will be unsure about the source of the defendant's products or whether the plaintiff endorsed them.

(3) Similarity of marks—If the overall impression created by the plaintiff's mark or the general use of his identity are similar or strongly resemble the marks used by the defendant in terms of appearance, sound or meaning, there is a greater chance of consumer confusion.

(4) Evidence of actual confusion—While evidence of actual confusion is not necessary for a plaintiff to prevail, if a plaintiff can demonstrate actual confusion on the part of consumers, his case will be greatly strengthened. To do so, plaintiffs will often distribute surveys to the public that ask whether they associate the plaintiff with the defendant's product or whether they believe the plaintiff has endorsed the defendant's product.

(5) Marketing channels used—If the plaintiff's and defendant's goods and services will be marketed and sold in the same stores, or if they will be advertised in the same media, there is a greater chance of consumer confusion.

(6) Likely degree of purchaser care—If the targeted consumers are more sophisticated and prudent in their purchases, there is a smaller chance the court will find that a likelihood of confusion exists.

(7) Defendant's intent in selecting mark—If the plaintiff can demonstrate that the defendant knowingly used the plaintiff's mark or identity, it is more likely that a court will find the defendant did so willingly to derive benefit from the reputation of the plaintiff. While such a showing is not required to prevail, it suggests an intent to cause a likelihood of confusion.

(8) Likelihood of expansion of product lines—If the products of the plaintiff and defendant differ, a court will consider how likely it is that the plaintiff will begin selling the products for which the defendant is using plaintiff's mark. The

higher that possibility, the greater the likelihood of confusion.

Courts have emphasized that these factors create no precise mathematical formula and that a plaintiff does not have to prove all or even most to succeed. Rather, these factors serve as subjective aids for determining the likelihood that consumers will be misled or confused about the athlete's sponsorship or approval of the product or service. The following examples help illustrate how these factors are treated in actual cases:

- Famous singer Tom Waits brought suit against Frito–Lay, Inc. for featuring a voice in their radio commercials that imitated Waits' signature raspy voice. The district court found, and the Ninth Circuit affirmed, that Frito–Lay had intentionally targeted its commercial to an audience that overlapped with Waits' audience. Additionally, Waits presented evidence of actual consumer confusion by presenting witnesses who believed it was Tom Waits singing the words of endorsement. As a result, the court found there to be sufficient evidence that consumers were likely to be misled by the commercial into believing that Waits endorsed Frito–Lay's product. *Waits v. Frito–Lay, Inc.*, 978 F.2d 1093 (9th Cir. 1992).

- Defendant Men's World Outlet used celebrity look-alikes of Woody Allen in store advertisements that were run in Newsweek. Woody Allen brought suit under the Lanham Act for false endorsement and false association. Applying the likelihood of confusion test, the court found that Allen's mark as a famous film creator and actor was very strong and the look-alike created a substantial similarity between the two marks. It further found that Newsweek, as a general-interest tabloid, would not have readers sophisticated about film, which increased the likelihood of confusion. Finally, the court analyzed conversations of defendants that indicated that they were aware of Woody Allen's mark and, at the least, created the advertisement to invoke an association with the plaintiff. For these reasons, Allen prevailed. *Allen v. Men's World Outlet*, 679 F. Supp. 360 (S.D.N.Y. 1988).

- Robotic figures resembling famous members of the "Cheers" cast were placed outside airport bars modeled after the famous set of the television show. In response, two of the actors brought suit under the Lanham Act. The Ninth Circuit reversed the district court's granting of summary judgment for defendants by discussing the viability of all eight factors of the likelihood of confusion test: (1) because the actors were members of a famous television show, their mark is arguably strong, (2) the goods of the actors (fame as actors) are related to the bar's goods (the drinks, food, etc.) in that the source of both of their fame is the Cheers television show, (3) the robots are arguably similar to the likeness of the actors, (4) the plaintiffs provided survey evidence of consumer confusion, (5) the target audience of the bar is customers who have watched Cheers, (6) bar customers are less likely to carefully consider whether the actors endorse the product, (7) there is evidence that defendants intended to design the figures to imitate the actors and (8) one of the actors had considered large-scale beer endorsements for the future. *Wendt v. Host Int'l, Inc.*, 125 F.3d 806 (9th Cir. 1997).

- Twentieth Century Fox Films licensed a toy company, Galoob, the rights to produce and market a line of "Predator" toys based on their feature film. William Landham, an actor in the movie, filed a false endorsement claim under Section 43(a) of the Lanham Act for a Micro Machine toy named "Bill" that stood 1.5 inches tall and lacked eyes or a mouth. Applying the factors in Fox's favor, the court noted that the adult nature of Landham's work made it unlikely that his mark had any strength among child toy purchasers, that the marks were far from similar, that the defendant's intent was lacking, and there was no risk of Landham expanding into the toy production industry. *Landham v. Lewis Galoob Toys, Inc.*, 227 F.3d 619 (6th Cir. 2000).

- In 1998, artist Rick Rush created a painting entitled "The Masters of Augusta," which was designed to commemorate Tiger Woods's victory at the Masters golf tournament. The painting featured Woods in three different poses. To his left was his caddy and in the background were the likenesses of other great Masters champions. In addition to their publicity rights infringement claims, the plaintiffs also claimed violations of the Lanham Act for the unauthorized use of the likeness of Tiger Woods and for falsely implying that Woods had endorsed the painting.

  In response to these claims, the court first held that as a general rule, a person's image or likeness cannot function as a trademark. In response to the second claim, the court ruled that in "Lanham Act false endorsement cases involving artistic expression, the likelihood of confusion test does not give sufficient weight to the public interest in free expression." As a result, the court held that the Lanham Act and the likelihood of confusion test should only be applied when the public interest in avoiding confusion outweighs the public interest in free expression.

Alternatively, the dissent argued that while a balancing test between avoiding confusion and protecting expression is appropriate, the analysis should include consideration of the eight factors. Specifically, the dissent pointed to a survey conducted by the plaintiffs that indicated that 62% had answered "yes" to the question: "Do you believe that Tiger Woods has an affiliation or connection with this print or that he has given his approval or has sponsored it?" *ETW Corp. v. Jireh Publishing, Inc.*, 332 F.3d 915 (6th Cir. 2003)

C. *Defenses to a Right of Publicity Infringement Claim*

The previous section has identified the major state and federal right of publicity infringement claims that an athlete may make against persons infringing his rights. This section focuses on the variety of defenses asserted by allegedly infringing users. Besides attacking the normal elements comprising a publicity rights claim, an alleged offender will likely raise a host of other defenses that are discussed below. Due to the unsettled nature of the law in this field, nearly any one could prove successful. As such, the athlete's representative should understand these arguments and be prepared to combat each in turn. The most wide-ranging First Amendment defenses will be addressed first.

First Amendment Defenses

The First Amendment is generally seen to expansively protect all forms of expression, traditional and novel. The Restatement (Third) of Unfair Competition, in a comment to its definition of the right of publicity, states that the right "as recognized by statute and common law is fundamentally constrained by the public and constitutional interest in freedom of expression."[78] Thus the law promotes achieving a balance or drawing a line between the right of publicity and freedom of expression in certain instances. As such, courts usually attempt to weigh the competing interests of publicity and free speech and determine which seems stronger in a particular case. Unfortunately, the Supreme Court has not provided a specific method to accomplish this task. Incorporating ideas from more developed fields with similar underlying policies (such as copyright and trademark law) has proven helpful but also confusing because the doctrines do not perfectly translate to publicity rights. This has led to an interrelated collection of doctrines inconsistently adopted by different jurisdictions across the country. The breadth of First Amendment limitations upon publicity rights and their inconsistent

---

78. Restatement (Third) of Unfair Competition § 47, *Comment c.*

application by the courts means that alleged infringers will attempt a variety of "free expression" defenses.

Though rarely applied now, a "merchandise vs. media" distinction appeared historically in publicity rights cases. Under this test the medium dominated, not the message, such that traditional merchandise such as coffee mugs and T-shirts did not qualify for First Amendment protection while traditional media such as paintings or plays could trump publicity rights. Courts permitted the sale of comments about a celebrity, but not anything that appeared to sell the celebrity themselves. Because of the influx of new forms of media in recent decades, courts have departed from this test.

Commercial Speech

The Supreme Court has made it clear that the First Amendment looks beyond the medium of expression, thus extending its reach past written and spoken words to paintings, plays, sculptures, music, and other non-traditional methods of expression. However, the Constitution does not safeguard all forms of "speech." For instance, the First Amendment does not cover false or misleading speech and commercial speech receives only limited protection. The Supreme Court has defined commercial speech as "expression related solely to the economic interests of the speaker and its audience;"[79] for example, advertisements generally epitomize the purest form of commercial speech. According to *Gionfriddo v. Major League Baseball*, advertisements violate the right of publicity when "the plaintiff's identity is used, without consent, to promote an unrelated product."[80] The more unrelated the relevant product is to the appropriated identity, the less constitutional protection the expression will receive. Generally speech is thought to exist on a spectrum where on one end purely non-commercial speech receives the highest protection and on the other wholly commercial speech garners much less, though still significant, protection. By demonstrating that a particular expression does not warrant full First Amendment support, a plaintiff can potentially defeat or at least weaken a defendant's freedom of expression argument.

Fair Use

Because the *Zachinni* opinion in the same sentence discussed the First Amendment's reach into both publicity rights and copyright, several courts have borrowed from copyright law when confronted with a publicity rights case. Incorporation of the "fair use" doctrine has become particularly popular. The doctrine requires the weighing of four factors to determine if a use is "fair" and thus not

79. *Bolger v. Youngs Drug Products Corp.*, 463 U.S. 60, 66 (1983).

80. *Central Hudson Gas & Elec. Corp. v. Public Serv. Comm'n*, 447 U.S. 557, 561 (1980).

a copyright violation: (1) the purpose and character of the use (*e.g.,* is it a permissible "educational use" of previously copyrighted material?), (2) the nature of the copyrighted work being taken, (3) the amount and substantiality of the portion used in relation to the copyrighted work as a whole, and (4) the effect of the use upon the potential market for or value of the copyrighted work. As applied to publicity rights, the second and third factors do not appear to translate well because both will simply consist of an individual's identity. However, for better or worse courts have found the two remaining factors helpful in navigating the unsettled field of publicity rights. Hence many courts when attempting a First Amendment versus publicity rights balancing test will primarily scrutinize (1) the purpose of the appropriated use and (2) the effect of that use upon the market for the celebrity's likeness.

News and Fact Dissemination

The dissemination of news and historical fact has become the most widely-accepted First Amendment defense to a publicity rights infringement claim. Courts widely agree that the public has a strong interest in the spreading of news and information and that this interest can at times supersede the right of publicity. Though the Supreme Court in *Zachinni* held that the press cannot without consent broadcast a performer's entire act, it specifically noted that the performer's right of publicity could not prevent someone from reporting the newsworthy facts about the act.[81] For example, the Second Circuit allowed a commercial magazine to advertise itself on the side of buses using Mayor Rudy Giuliani's name.[82] Thus even for-profit news providers will generally escape liability from publicity rights infringement when they appropriate names or likenesses in connection with a specific story or their reporting generally. However, determining whether or not one's purpose was to disseminate information can become a contested issue.

The oft-cited *Gionfriddo* holding permitted Major League Baseball to display on its website historical information such as rosters, box scores, game summaries, and memorable video clips because in the court's opinion such items amounted to "mere bits of baseball's history . . . [and entertainment] features receive the same constitutional protection as factual news reports."[83] The court determined that MLB had acted to further education in and spread information about baseball, an important part of the country's culture. Disseminating historical facts, however, will not always suffice to obtain

81. *See Zacchini v. Scripps–Howard Broadcasting Co.,* 433 U.S. 562, 574 (1977).

82. *Metropolitan Transportation Auth. v. New York Magazine,* 119 S. Ct. 68 (1998) (memorandum).

83. *Gionfriddo v. Major League Baseball,* 114 Cal. Rptr. 2d 307, 314 (2001) (citing 433 U.S. 562).

First Amendment protection. Two important publicity rights cases, *Palmer v. Schonhorn Enterprises, Inc.* and *Uhlaender v. Henricksen*, both found violations of publicity rights when parties sold board games featuring athletes' biographical information and performance statistics. Similarities can be drawn between these two cases and MLB's actions in *Gionfriddo*. However, MLB used once-licensed information and video it helped create to promote professional baseball, whereas the defendants in *Palmer* and *Uhlaender* appear less sympathetic because they appropriated identities to market unrelated products. One imagines the *Gionfriddo* court would not have treated a random entrepreneur as kindly. Generally an enterprise will have to demonstrate that providing information is its primary purpose to qualify for First Amendment protection of news and fact dissemination.

Public Domain Not a Defense

The defendants in *Palmer* and *Uhlaender* did not claim protection for spreading facts. Instead they attempted to escape liability by arguing that the appropriated information was already in the public domain and thus free to use. Importantly, both courts held the voluntary disclosure of information through news media did not extinguish the athletes' rights and that information in the public domain remains subject to publicity rights. The *Uhlaender* opinion noted that a name is "commercially valuable as an endorsement of a product or for use for financial gain only because the public recognizes it and attributes good will and feats of skill or accomplishments of one sort or another to that personality."[84] Consequently public domain, although similar in many ways to fair use, will not trump the right of publicity.

Parody

The courts have decided entertaining speech deserves as much constitutional protection as informing speech. Additionally, the United States has always vigorously safeguarded the right to social commentary. Consequently, the practice of "parody" has obtained full First Amendment protection. Though parody has arisen only a few times in publicity rights, its protection in other fields requiring First Amendment balancing is well-established. *Cardtoons v. Major League Baseball Players Association*,[85] where a company produced baseball cards featuring easily recognizable caricatures rather than players' real names and pictures, represents the seminal parody case with respect to publicity rights. The defendant in the case had clearly appropriated the identity of professional baseball players but

84. *Uhlaender*, 316 F. Supp. 1277 at 1283.

85. *Cardtoons, L.C. v. Major League Baseball Players Association*, 95 F.3d 959 (10th Cir. 1996).

had provided humorous and arguably insightful commentary through its transformation of each individual athlete. After weighing Cardtoons' parody as a "vital commodity in the marketplace of ideas,"[86] the court examined the effect of infringing upon the publicity rights. It stated that unlike other types of appropriation, parody does not seem to provide celebrities with any additional income because rarely, if ever, will a celebrity give permission for a parody of him or herself. The court noted that parody rarely acts as a substitute for an original work and thus does not economically affect the market for non-parodist works. Additionally, the market for parodies is small enough that the court felt celebrities would not lose incentive to enter their respective fields. Finally, and perhaps most importantly, the court expressed concern that celebrities given control of their appropriation in parodies would "use that power to suppress criticism, and thus permanently remove a valuable source of information about their identity from the marketplace."[87] Historically the law has held sacrosanct the freedom of individuals to openly mock public figures. The potential chilling of speech caused by allowing the MLBPA to censor criticism of itself was deemed "clearly undesirable." In conclusion the court summarized the balancing by stating that little was to be gained and much lost from protecting the athletes' publicity rights in this instance.

Transformative Effect

In a cursory discussion of non-economic considerations (noted but not adopted), the *Cardtoons* court mentioned that far from being a lazy copier, the defendant had added a significant creative component to the athletes' identities and thus created a new work rather than simply obtaining an unjust enrichment. This creative element of products featuring appropriated celebrity identities, coined the "transformative use" in fair use, has become its own First Amendment defense to publicity rights claims. Articulated by the California Supreme Court in *Comedy III Productions, Inc. v. Gary Saderup, Inc.*,[88] and adopted by the Sixth Circuit in *ETW Corp. v. Jireh Publishing, Inc.*,[89] the transformative use doctrine gives First Amendment protection to expression that has added significant creativity to an appropriation of identity. The California Supreme Court summarized the test as "whether the celebrity likeness is one of the 'raw materials' from which an original work is synthesized, or whether the depiction or imitation of the celebrity is the very sum and substance of the work in question."[90] To receive protection, the defendant must transform the product featuring the celebrity likeness to the extent that the expression becomes primar-

---

86. *Cardtoons*, 95 F.3d 959 at 972.

87. *Id.* at 975.

88. 25 Cal. 4th 387 (2001).

89. 332 F. 3d 915 (6th Cir. 2003).

90. 25 Cal. 4th 387 at 406.

ily the defendant's. The artistic creativity is added to the First Amendment side of the scale balancing publicity rights versus freedom of expression. For example, artist Rick Rush created paintings commemorating Tiger Woods' first Masters victory featuring multiple depictions of Woods on the Augusta National course. Though the images of Woods occupied most of the picture, the Sixth Circuit refused to find a violation of Woods' publicity rights because it believed that "Rush's work consists of a collage of images in addition to Woods' image which are combined to describe, in artistic form, a historic event in sports history and to convey a message about the significance of Woods' achievement in that event."[91] The court concluded that the substantial creative and informative content of Rush's work outweighed Woods' right to his publicity. Despite being relatively new to the publicity rights sphere, the transformative use test has begun to gain traction in various jurisdictions. And while it can provide assistance in a First Amendment balancing exercise, the test's attempts to measure "creativity" probably ensure the law will remain murky and unclear.

Celebrities Make Enough Money

Most celebrities with identities worth appropriating enjoy significant financial success. Consequently, courts will often feel less sympathy toward a celebrity than to an apparently hard-working entrepreneur and, when balancing the First Amendment against the right of publicity, will take into account the celebrity's already established ability to reap financial reward from his identity. Considering the effect the infringement would have on the celebrity's ability to profit from his identity allows courts to arguably incorporate a non-economic argument into publicity rights, which are "supposedly" purely economic. For example, the Sixth Circuit in *Jireh* minimized the alleged infringement's effects because Tiger Woods could realize a large profit without exploiting his right of publicity in lithograph posters. Additionally, the court did not believe that Rick Rush's painting would reduce the commercial value of Woods' likeness. Because the right of publicity arose to allow public figures to extract the value of their likeness, it seems odd that courts would allow infringement when celebrities "can make their money elsewhere." However, this line of thinking often appears in court-conducted analysis.

Tests Borrowed From Trademark Law

Judges facing publicity rights issues have also incorporated trademark law when analyzing First Amendment defenses. These tests have not commonly appeared, but remain relevant and thus worth noting. They include the relatedness test, the alternative means test, and the merchandise versus media test.

---

91.   332 F. 3d 915 at 938.

Occasionally courts have used a "relatedness" test advocated by the Restatement (Third) of Unfair Competition to determine the permissibility of expressive appropriation of celebrity identities. This test precludes publicity rights liability if the relevant appropriated rights relate to the work and classifies as infringing those that use the likeness solely to attract attention to a work unrelated to the identified person.[92] It bears some resemblance to the commercial speech analysis.

An "alternative means" test has been mentioned but not yet adopted in publicity rights cases. Used to strike a balance between property rights and free speech, the alternative means test inquires whether adequate alternative means were available that would not invade property rights. Alternative means does not appear to translate well to publicity rights claims and the *Cardtoons* court stated that in the context of intellectual property the test did not sufficiently value the public's interest in free expression.

Other Defenses

Copyright Preemption

The Copyright Act may preempt a right of publicity claim in instances where a party brings forth a claim that could be brought under federal copyright law. The California Court of Appeals explained that preemption occurs when:

1. The subject matter of the claim is a work fixed in a tangible medium of expression and comes within the subject matter or scope of copyright protection as described under the Copyright Act, and

2. The right asserted under state law is equivalent to the exclusive rights contained in § 106 of the Copyright Act.[93]

More concisely, so long as a plaintiff claims infringement of personal, state-law rights distinct from those protected by copyright, they can avoid preemption. For example, baseball players attempting to acquire the rights to their performances in a televised broadcast of a game were prohibited from pursing publicity rights claims because the telecasts were fixed in a tangible form and thus the domain of copyright law.[94] However, other Copyright Act cases have also interpreted the "likeness" or "identity" element of state publicity rights statutes to represent a persona that cannot become fixed in any tangible medium and as such have declined to find copyright preemption.

92. *See, e.g., Seale v. Gramercy Pictures*, 949 F.Supp. 331, 336 (E.D. Pa. 1996).

93. *KNB Enterprises v. Matthews*, 78 Cal. App. 4th 362 (2000).

94. *Baltimore Orioles, Inc. v. Major League Baseball Players Ass'n*, 805 F. 2d 663 (7th Cir. 1986).

First Sale Doctrine

Representing another idea borrowed from copyright law, the first sale doctrine prevents an intellectual property right holder from allowing the sale of copies and later exercising the distribution right with respect to those copies. In a sense the first sale of a product featuring an appropriated identity "exhausts" the celebrity's publicity rights in that particular copy of the product. For example, Vintage Sports Plaques successfully invoked the first sale doctrine to defend its business of purchasing trading cards, packaging them together with frames and plaques, and selling them to the public.[95] To find this activity infringing, as noted by the court, would have a disastrous effect on industries revolving around the resale of goods.

Posthumous Publicity Rights

In certain jurisdictions demonstrating that a celebrity died will suffice to defend a publicity rights infringement claim. A few states reserve postmortem publicity rights for 50 years, 100 years, or even arguably perpetually, but the majority of jurisdictions appear to prohibit the assertion of publicity rights to the heirs or assignees of deceased public figures. Therefore checking in which state a deceased celebrity claimed to have been domiciled will provide a critical component in any publicity rights dispute.

Chapter 4, Section C—Questions for Discussion

Now please use the foregoing considerations to address the following litigation "hypothetical."

1. When Negotiating a License Agreement Breaks Down: The Hypothetical

For purposes of the following litigation hypothetical, familiarize yourself with the facts in the previous Freddy Flair hypothetical following Section B of this Chapter. Then, assume the following additional facts:

1. The Negotiation Breaks Down, as Freddy Flair Learns New Facts: The negotiation between Golfer ("Woody") and Artist ("Freddy Flair") has broken down over the following issues:

    a. Woody wants to exert too much "control" over Freddy's "final pre-production rendering." In response, Freddy only can say, "It is what it is. Take it or leave it. I can only be inspired by a magical moment one time. I need to tell my digital reproduction story as I see it. I, like you, Woody, can't get a 'Mulligan' to try to 'do over' the most important swing photo I've every digitally reproduced."

---

95. *Allison   v.   Vintage   Sports Plaques*, 136 F. 3d 1443 (11th Cir. 1998).

b. In response, however, Woody's attorney advises Freddy's attorney as follows: Freddy's "collage" photo of Woody's "signature swing finish" infringes on Woody's previously marketed Nike poster of that same pose. In fact, Woody's attorney informs Freddy's attorney that, as part of Woody's mega-endorsement deal with Nike, the "poster category" has already been "sold" to Nike, including the right to use Woody's distinctive "swing finish" in that category.

c. Thus, Freddy now knows that if he proceeds to go to market with his collage "as is," Nike and/or Woody will claim that Freddy is thereby "stealing" a pre-sold category from Woody, for which Nike/Woody will be seeking compensatory and punitive damages relating to, inter alia, negatively impacting Nike's post-Major rollout of its "campaign" for Woody-endorsed Nike products.

> This campaign relies heavily on the accompanying use of the "signature swing" image in Nike's current poster. (N.B. Nike also owns (per its contract with Woody) the "signature swing finish" image for purposes of branding/selling other Nike products (beyond posters) including products in the category of original art work for limited edition oil paintings to be created by high-end Leroy Neiman-type sports artists if/when Nike deems it most appropriate to exploit that category.)

2. <u>Freddy Takes Some Well–Deserved Time Off</u>: In light of the foregoing, to avoid a mega-damages lawsuit for "interference" with Woody's current Nike agreement, Freddy decides against marketing his current product and wishes Woody well during the upcoming PGA season.

3. <u>Freddy Becomes Inspired Again</u>: As the next PGA Tour season begins, and the anniversary of Woody's first Major approaches, Freddy is compelled to go back into his "creative mode." In so doing, he decides to "start all over again," with a new "inspiration" for his digitally reproduced Woody/Major "creation."

> Out of respect for his Muse, however, Freddy simply claims that the new creation will demonstrate his most distinctive "Flair" ever. He also announces that it will be accompanied by an appropriately modified title to reflect his new inspiration, which will be unveiled at the time of the Major.

      a.   In reply, Woody's attorney advises Nike accordingly. Woody/Nike immediately retain the law firm of KOKO ("Knock Out Knock Offs"), to watch the market for a flood of Freddy's new product.

   4.   <u>Freddy's New Creation is Unveiled at the Major</u>: As Woody prepares to defend his title, KOKO is patrolling the Major course's premises during the Wednesday practice round. On public property, near the only driveway entrance where all PGA Tour officials, media, players, and fans must enter the premises, KOKO discovers Freddy Flair "setting up shop," with five to six helpers promoting the "exclusive" sale of hundreds of the following (variously sized), product: the same digitally reproduced collage that Woody had refused to license to Freddy a year ago, subject only to the following distinctive "Flairs":

      a.   The photo of Woody's "signature swing finish" has been "touched up" by Freddy to slightly reposition Woody's head so that Woody appears to be looking beyond the 18th green (where his parents await him), rather than tracking the flight of the ball.

      b.   Also, in the third time-sequenced photo in the collage, Freddy has "touched up" the photo to reposition Woody's head to make it appear as if Woody is looking back at his last shot to the green, instead of looking at his parents.

Inspired by his new creation, Freddy has also retitled his digital reproduction: "WOODY's Home Hole." (Emphasis supplied by Freddy, for artistic effect.)

Please consult the Teacher's Manual for the most creative solutions to this "hypothetical" pre-litigation scenario.

So, too, in the following "publicity rights" scenario, should you consider the following "hypothetical," to which "sample answers" are provided in the Teacher's Manual.

2. *Determining Who Owns Media Rights: The Hypothetical*

PGA Player ("Player") is a member of the PGA Tour, who is governed by the terms of the PGA handbook, to which he has agreed. Those terms should be assumed to include, for purposes of this Hyothetical, the following provisions:

Section V(B)(1)(a) and (b) of the PGA Tour Player Handbook:

1) Media Rights

(a) The television, radio, motion picture and all other media rights of all players participating in PGA TOUR cosponsored and coordinated tournaments, pro-ams or any other golf event conducted in conjunction with PGA TOUR cosponsored and coordinated tournaments (e.g., clinics, long-drive contests), or any portion thereof, shall be granted and assigned to PGA TOUR. Based upon this grant and assignment, all such rights shall be the property of and expressly reserved by and to PGA TOUR, and any use thereof without the express written consent of PGA TOUR shall be forbidden.

Section V(B)(2)(a) and (b) of the PGA Tour Player Handbook:

2) Marketing Rights

(a) Aside from the assignment of individual television and similar rights provided for herein, nothing in these Regulations or in marketing programs adopted by PGA TOUR shall be deemed to restrict any member's individual marketing rights (e.g., promotions, endorsements, licensing, etc.).

(b) In addition, no person shall make any commercial use of the name, likeness or identity of any member of PGA TOUR without the advance written approval of such member.

(c) Similarly, no individual PGA TOUR member, tournament sponsor or other person or entity is authorized to make any commercial use of the PGA TOUR name.

Given the controlling language, assume the following background facts for this hypothetical involving Player's participation on the PGA tour:

1. Player wins his first PGA Tour victory in Las Vegas in Year 1. Player has just recently turned pro and has signed a number of multi-year off-course endorsement agreements, upon joining the PGA Tour. Player has not, however, yet won a "Major" championship, which is his self-described career goal.

2. In Year 2 of his PGA career, he very much wants to defend his Las Vegas PGA tournament victory in Year 1. However, he is being more strategic in thinking about in which events he should play to match up with his "open" endorsement categories, which include: (1) the golf course design category; (2) the "resort and/or casino" category; and (3) the "putter" category in his golf club endorsement agreement.

3. On the assumption that Player will want to defend his title in Year 2, the PGA and the sponsor of the Las Vegas tournament (the Las Vegas Convention and Visitors Bureau—"LCVB") have embarked on a promotional campaign to attract visitors to Las Vegas in general and, in particular, to the LCVB PGA tournament event in Year 2 of Player's PGA career.

4. In connection with that promotion, and by taking advantage of the PGA's "media rights" rule (quoted above), the LCVB has, with the PGA's approval, in consideration for the LCVB's payment to the PGA of its event sanction fee, taken the following action: it has constructed, without Player's prior approval, a large billboard near the Las Vegas Airport, which features Player's "fist pump" captured in a PGA-owned photo while sinking the winning putt at the Las Vegas Tour event in Year 1. The billboard contains the following message, "Welcome to Las Vegas!"

    No mention is made in the billboard, however, of the PGA Tour or the upcoming PGA event, which is scheduled to start in four weeks. (The LCVB has paid for the construction of the billboard and plans to continue to run Player's image as part of this billboard ad for the next two months, at an expense of approximately $10,000 per month.)

5. Superimposed in the background behind Player's image is an image of Las Vegas' most recently opened resort (the "Wind Resort") including the Wind Resort's lavish casino gambling hall and the inviting "first tee" of its privately owned resort golf course, which has been designed by Golden Bear Design Co. (Jack Nicklaus's Company), and which course recently opened to the public with Nicklaus's playing a highly publicized "first round" with "founding members" of the Club.

6. The LCVB's billboard ad claims to be simply advertising Las Vegas as a "destination resort" where championship PGA Tour golf is played and where the best players in the world come both to golf and to try their hand at casino gambling while staying at a lavish resort, etc.

7. Player's agent was not notified of the billboard until after it had been constructed, by which time Player had already tentatively agreed to participate in Year 2 of the Las Vegas event, because he wants to defend his title.

8. The LCVB has now decided to run a nationwide ad in USA Today, in both its hard copy and digital format, as well as on its Tour event website, using this same billboard ad, again with the PGA's permission but without Player's

consent, by the PGA's relying upon the PGA's "media rights" rules, quoted above.

The only difference in the USA Today ad, as opposed to the billboard, is that Player's putter's brand ("Odyssey"), for which Player is currently not being compensated, is clearly visible in the USA Today ad's PGA-owned photo of Player's final winning putt.

9. On the Monday before the LCVB Tournament is set to begin, the LCVB decides to run this ad on Wednesday and Thursday before the Las Vegas event and wants to add only the following tag-line: "Watch Player defend his Las Vegas title this weekend on the XYZ network," with the hours of the television broadcast listed below the tag-line.

10. Player claims that his "marketing rights" under the PGA rules have been infringed, both by the construction of the billboard and certainly by the proposed ad in USA Today. On the Monday prior to the LCVB Tournament, Player and his agent/attorney must decide whether to go to court to seek a preliminary injunction to stop the running of the proposed ad, which is set to go to print later this week.

11. In response, PGA Tour/LCVB claim that, per the terms of the standard PGA Tour Entry Form, Player has also granted the Tour, inter alia, all of Player's "media rights" to be used in "(1) advertising, promoting or publicizing the PGA Tour, the tournament or any broadcasts thereof . . ."

Given the above, "you make the call." Who gets the better of the argument between the PGA/LCVB invoking the "media rights" rule (and the above-referenced Player Entry Form language) in promoting the Las Vegas tournament, etc., versus Player invoking the "marketing rights" rules to prevent the continued running of the billboard and the proposed running of the USA Today advertisement?

In considering these questions, consider what "products or categories" the PGA/LCVB may be infringing in Player's future endorsement career, on the assumption that he does not yet have a golf course design or "resort destination," or "putter" product endorsement, but will be seeking them over the course of his career.

In an attempt to resolve these matters amicably, similarly consider the possibility of "soft money" being paid to Player and/or his family and/or his Foundation as an inducement to get Player to participate in the Las Vegas tournament.

Finally, consider whether the possibility of lending Player's name to a new casino and/or golf course development in Las Vegas would be a further appropriate inducement for LCVB to offer Player and his agent/attorney.

Negotiating/Drafting of Proposed "Cease and Desist"/"Intent to Sue" Letter and Response Thereto

In your sub-Group, prepare to negotiate the above-described Hypothetical for 35–45 minutes,[96] and begin to draft a "cease and desist" or "intent to sue" letter on behalf of Player.

The other sub-Group should prepare a negotiation response to same on behalf of the PGA Tour/LCVB and, in so doing, should begin to draft a proposed response to Player, making use of the "media rights" rule read in conjunction with the Player Entry Form signed by Player in Year 1.

Negotiating/Drafting of Proposed Settlement

After negotiating such "intent to sue" letter or response thereto for 5–10 minutes, you will re-group in your sub-Group. In so doing, you should consider what form of proposed "settlement agreement" could resolve all issues among the Player, the PGA Tour and the LCVB. Begin to draft same, while continuing the "settlement agreement" negotiation for the first 20–25 minutes of class.

Per usual, please see the Teacher's Manual for "exemplar" responses to this multi-faceted pre-litigation hypothetical fact scenario.

D. *The Future of Publicity Rights*

Technological advances over the last few decades, particularly with respect to computers and the Internet, have given rise to countless new media and products. More people communicate and continuously do so in novel fashions. This constant innovation brings with it new methods of appropriating celebrity identities and thus new manners of infringement. The developing applications of publicity rights further muddle the state of the legal field and promise to offer challenges in the years to come.

Increased sophistication and power in computer programming allow artists to manipulate and in some sense create celebrity photos. Morphing existing pictures into new ones with alternative clothing, setting, or bodies can result in an entirely different picture. A magazine discussing Hollywood's evolution that had altered famous celebrity photos (including Dustin Hoffman, John Travolta, and Elvis Presley) to "dress" the various actors and

---

96. In so doing, reverse roles so that if you last represented Player, you should represent the PGA Tour/LCVB, and vice versa.

actresses in contemporary designer clothes escaped liability for publicity rights infringement because the court concluded the images were noncommercial speech presented without malice.[97] In addition, computer-generated imaging has advanced to a level capable of creating two- and three-dimensional characters that clearly resemble known celebrities. Video games are now advanced products that will appropriate identities to add realism.

Disputes relating to the Internet offer a glimpse of the publicity rights issues that will arise in the near future. During the Internet's early days and to an extent today individuals would cheaply register celebrity names as domain names and attempt to sell the right to the celebrity at a premium, a practice known as "cyber-squatting." The Anticybersquatting Consumer Protection Act has somewhat mitigated this threat by prohibiting a person from registering a domain name that consists of or strongly resembles the name of another living person if their specific purpose is to profit from the exercise by selling the domain name. However, an administrative panel refused to award Eddie Van Halen the rights to edwardvanhalen.com when the panel found no evidence of bad faith and that the total lack of content on the website could be attributed to reasonable delay.

Case law indicates that courts will apply the First Amendment to the Internet as vigorously as they do to off-line media and hence most names and pictures do not infringe rights of publicity under the news and fact dissemination doctrine. The flexible nature of the Internet has further blurred the distinctions between innovation, creativity, news-reporting, and exploitation. One particularly difficult emerging area is fantasy sports. Essentially in fantasy you become an "owner" or manager of a team composed of real players that you and the other owners of the league "draft" or select at the beginning of the season. How those players perform in real games over the course of the season determines how well you do in your fantasy league. Fantasy games have existed for years, but widespread Internet access has caused an explosion in their popularity and they continue to grow each year. To offer the games, however, fantasy service providers must display on their websites each player's name and his or her performance.

In the first tried case regarding ownership of fantasy statistics, *CBC v. MLB Advanced Media*,[98] the Eighth Circuit concluded that First Amendment interests superseded the infringement upon players' rights of publicity. The court determined that the players had successfully made out a cause a action for violation of their publici-

---

97. *Hoffman v. Capital Cities/ABC, Inc.*, 255 F. 3d 1180 (9th Cir. 2001).

98. *C.B.C. Distrib. and Mktg., Inc. v. Major League Baseball Advanced Media, L.P.*, 505 F. 3d 818 (8th Cir. 2007).

ty rights under Missouri law by demonstrating that the fantasy service had without consent appropriated the players' identities to obtain a commercial benefit. However, balancing First Amendment interests with the encroached-upon rights revealed mitigating factors, including that (1) the relevant information already resided in the public domain; (2) there was public value in information about baseball, "the national pastime;" (3) the infringement had a minimal effect on major league players' incentives because they already receive handsome compensation for their services; and (4) the appropriation would not mislead consumers because it did not create the illusion of endorsement. The court found the scales to tip in favor of First Amendment interests and thus refused to hold the fantasy provider liable. The aftermath of *CBC* will surely witness Internet entrepreneurs pushing the holding to its limits and exploring to discover at what point courts will find infringement.

Chapter 4, Section D—Questions for Discussion and Group Negotiation/Drafting Exercises

1. Fantasy Baseball & Multimedia: The Hypothetical

Consider the following "hypothetical" in the context of the foregoing analysis:

1. Assume that CBC has created its own baseball fantasy online game, which CBC League players can access while the player's Team is "playing" its games.

2. Assume further that the CBC fantasy baseball site provides asynchronous streaming of the real-time statistical performance of the Team's players.

3. Assume further that as a Team's player "scores points" for the Team by, e.g., hitting a home run, the CBC website creates a digitally enhanced image of the player in question to highlight the player's performance, together with the player's updated statistics based thereon. (This "image" takes the form of a "parody" of the player's actual image, plus a creative "nickname" for the player, such as "Clammy Sosa.")

4. Finally, assume that on the CBC fantasy game website, the following two (2) ads appear:

   a. One ad is for a CBC wholly owned travel agency affiliate. The ad for this affiliate reads as follows: "CBC Fantasy Travel—the agency of choice for the fantasy players whose images appear on this CBC website."

      b. The second ad is for a wholly owned CBC technology company. The ad reads as follows: "CBC Technologies—the internet and multimedia provider of choice for the players whose images appear on this fantasy website."

5. Based on the foregoing hypothetical, break up into your sub-Groups and represent CBC for MLBPA/MLBAM, respectively.

6. Begin to negotiate and then draft a "cease and desist" letter on behalf of MLBPA/BAM, and a response thereto on behalf of the CBC.

Please use the Teacher's Manual to see additional variations on the "publicity rights" themes evoked by this hypothetical.

2. *Multimedia Rights & the PGA Tour: Hypothetical*

Assumed "Hypothetical" Facts for Group Negotiation and Drafting Exercises

Similarly, in light of the legal principles described in this chapter, consider this additional hypothetical, to test the depth of your understanding of this critical area of professional athlete representation.

Assume that the same media rights and marketing rights quoted in hypothetical No. 2 in the Chapter 4, Section C "Questions for Discussion" apply. Then assume the following fact pattern.

The PGA Tour has announced that it intends to create an on-line, interactive game called "Play with the Pros."

This game will be playable only while PGA-sanctioned Tour events are being played. The participant will only be able to play the game by logging onto the PGA's website and paying a per-tournament fee to "participate" in the tournament of his/her choice.

The way that the game will be played, after a player logs on, is as follows: the PGA will use its exclusive television feed for the Tournament and simultaneously video-stream it to its website. Through advanced, proprietary technology in which the PGA has invested many millions of dollars, it will allow the participant to follow along with the Player of his/her choice, as the tournament progresses.

The game will also allow each participant to watch his selected Player take a shot and then select a shot of his/her own, by manipulating a digital "stick figure" identified by the selected Player's name, taking into account the Player's current place in the tournament. The participant can thus computer-simulate a shot-by-shot competition in which he/she will be able to "play with the pro" of his choice and attempt to beat the pro during the tournament.

"Group Negotiation" Considerations

You make the call. Does this "Play with the Pros" interactive real-time video game conflict with the PGA Tour Player's right to exclusively control his "marketing rights" in the product categories of, inter alia, video games or "interactive media" or "personal website" rights?

Each Group should break into sub-Groups to consider the following facts. One sub-Group will represent the PGA Tour. The other sub-Group will represent "a top 10 Player" whose major "product categories" are sold, except for the "video game" and "website/interactive media" categories.

Does each Player control the rights to his performance and statistics, as he is competing in a PGA Tour event, or has he granted those rights to the PGA Tour in the media rights language and Player Entry Form language referenced above?

What rights does the Player control to broadcast his Tournament performance on his own website, rather than the PGA Tour's website, even if he does it on a time-delayed basis?

What if the PGA Tour's website "banner advertising" that appears on "Play with the Pros" creates a conflict with a product category in which the Player already has an exclusive product endorsement agreement?

Can the Player sell banner advertising for a competing product in the same category on his own website at the same time as he "video streams" his tournament performance, either simultaneously with the PGA Tour's "feed," or, as an accommodation to the Tour's "media rights," on a (slightly) time-delayed basis?

What "joint venture" win/win possibilities exist for the top ten players on the Tour in this context? How about the lower-end players, who have less leverage and would probably appreciate the exposure created by the PGA's proposed game as well as the banner-advertising associated therewith, which might create the impression that the banner advertisers have, in fact, endorsed the lower-ranking player?

Is there a "right of publicity" issue here for the low-end Tour players, in connection with the banner advertising? Or is any publicity good for such players' careers?

How about any amateurs that might be participating in the tournament? Would they lose their amateur eligibility if pay-per-view customers played against them in "Play with the Pros"?

Related Questions

What if the players at the high-end of the Tour rankings want to put on a specialty televised event, like Tiger Woods'/David Duval's "Battle at Bighorn," and allow viewers to "compete" against them on each of the Player's individual websites? Who controls which media and marketing rights re: such a proposed "product category?"

Sub–Group Drafting Assignment—"The Binding Letter of Intent"

After considering each of the foregoing facts and negotiating same, each sub-Group should separately begin to draft a "binding letter of intent," in an attempt to work out each of the possible conflicts raised by the foregoing hypothetical.

In so doing, each sub-Group should attempt to draft a proposed "deal point" agreement on each "material issue" that exists between Player and the PGA Tour. The draft Letter of Intent ("L.O.I.") should therefore contain all "material terms" from which a more formal Settlement Agreement could be drafted by, e.g., adding "boilerplate" language, etc.

The L.O.I. should be negotiated on a "confidential" basis, with the understanding that it will apply only to the Player in question. "Leverage points" should include, however, the precedential value of settling with one Player (or not), given the likelihood that additional challenges to the rules will soon follow from other "Top 10" Tour players.

Bonus Question: If time permits, the L.O.I. should also attempt to include a "once and for all resolution" in this area of "media rights, now known or hereafter devised," including a resolution of the "Monday Night Golf" type of dispute referenced in the Teacher's Manual.

Again, "exemplar" responses and sample Class Plans can be found to help guide the "interactive" explanations of this exciting and evolving area of "players' rights."[99]

99. See, for example, the recent widely publicized adverse ruling against the NFL Players Association in a case brought by a "class" of retired NFL players to enforce, *inter alia*, the retired players' "publicity rights," in EA/Madden video games.

Chapter 5

MANAGING THE MATURE ATHLETE

Thus far, this book has explored the representation of an athlete through a variety of career phases. Beginning with representation during the initial transformation from amateur to professional status and the fiduciary duties of the agent-player relationship. The subsequent chapters have detailed how player representatives negotiate product endorsements, secure licensing agreements and pursue litigation against infringers of the player's rights as the athlete's career develops. In this chapter, we will explore the considerations and strategies for representing the professional athlete at the end of his career. In doing so, we will briefly summarize a variety of substantive law areas that affect the athlete in his waning years.

Section A offers a brief introduction to the interface of the third and fourth stages of an athlete's career: maturity and decline. It discusses how agents should help structure their clients' endorsement deals and seek out new deals that will allow athletes to successfully transition into the post-athletic career stage. Sections B, C and D turn towards some of the legal issues that maturing athletes may face. Section B focuses on the substantive law surrounding whether or not athletes—both collegiate and professional—may secure workers' compensation benefits if injured on the job. Section C focuses on tort law, and particular tort law claims that aging athletes may want to make. Section D then concludes the chapter with an examination of an athlete's right to continue playing after incurring a disability.

"In Focus": Miscellaneous Factors to Be Considered in Counseling the "Maturing Athlete"

Throughout this Chapter, you will be studying the leading cases that can be used to counsel the maturing athlete in virtually every aspect of his career as the athlete nears retirement and contemplates post-retirement career options.

Using these cases, you should consider, for example, when it is appropriate (if ever) to "bite the hand that feeds," e.g. by filing a claim or a lawsuit against the athlete's current or former team/employer or union. In turn, if you advise the athlete to do so, you will need to counsel the athlete on the effect, positive or negative, that filing such a claim will have on the athlete's post-career endorsement opportunities and "publicity rights."

If your athlete-client becomes seriously injured, you will have to advise the athlete concerning what additional risks, if any, he should continue to assume, if to do so will, inter alia, permit the athlete to "vest" in his union's pension plan and/or to fulfill the athlete's off-field or off-course endorsement agreements' "must play" contractual obligations.

If an athlete's injury is misdiagnosed, either negligently or intentionally, you must consider what recourse, if any, the athlete might have against his team and/or its employed physicians. In so doing, the athlete's attorney must also consider what "malpractice" and other insurance policies might respond to make the athlete whole for the athlete's proximately caused damages.

Alternatively, if the athlete decides to continue to play after serious injury, or by "assuming the risk" of playing the athlete's sport, to what written or oral "waivers," if any, should the athlete agree? What if to do so will allow the athlete to prolong his career either with his current team or another team? In turn, if such prolongation fails, at what point will the athlete have forfeited his right to file a claim or to recover under a (permanent or temporary) "disability policy," if the athlete owns one either individually or through the athlete's union?[1]

In general, as to the maturing athlete's financial resources, before such final choices must be made, any potential post-retirement sources of income, including insurance policies, should be analyzed and firmed up, on the assumption that every play "could be the athlete's last."

Similarly, the athlete's investment portfolio should, if appropriate, be "recalibrated" to provide him with the greatest possible number of long-term, income-producing, income-replacement assets, until the athlete can (hopefully) bridge the post-career revenue generation gap into "life after sports" by pursuing a career in coaching, broadcasting, or, if possible, a non-sports career consistent with the athlete's pre-professional education.

---

1. Also, as to the aspiring pre-professional athlete, the question of injury and disability "waiver," will be considered in Section C below.

As the athlete's career matures, the athlete's attorney should also continue to ensure that all of the athlete's "affairs are in order" by, e.g., updating his last will and testament; ensuring that no contractually-binding documents or oral promises will come back to "haunt" the athlete in his retirement years; and drafting pre-or post-nuptial agreements, as may be necessary; etc.

By considering these and other factors highlighted throughout the cases in this Chapter, the athlete's attorney can proactively represent the client, to ensure the maximum number of income-producing opportunities for the athlete, as his career begins to come to a close.

One particular "hypothetical" example of the types of "go/no go" decisions that must be made by the "maturing" professional tennis athlete and the athlete's attorney is set forth below in Section A, to provide you with the opportunity to apply the lessons set forth in this Chapter and in prior sections of this book to the unique client challenges presented by an athlete nearing the end of his career. (As usual, "exemplar" response to this hypothetical are provided in the Teacher's Manual that accompanies this text.)

Other similar hypotheticals can be devised by "ringing the factual changes" on the legal themes illustrated by the cases summarized in this Chapter, to create the same type of "interactive" group negotiating and drafting assignments that are set forth throughout this book, to allow its readers to interactively use their "negotiating," "drafting," or "litigation voices," as the attorney's client's needs may require.

A.   *Marketing the Mature Athlete*

The average professional athlete will have a career lasting seven to twelve years. If he participates in a team sport, the average length drops to five years, and for contact sports like football, the average player competes less than four years. During that time, players on average will enjoy lifetime earnings somewhere between $5 million and $25 million—the majority of which will be earned before the player turns 35. If you compare these statistics to the average American worker who acquires lifetime earnings of $1 million to $3 million over the course of a 35– to 40– year career, it becomes clear that the professional career of an athlete is as transitory as it is lucrative.

In light of these characteristics, player representatives must carefully consider their client's long-term interests when securing endorsements and other marketing opportunities. While high-end players will attract endorsement deals from a wide range of big-

name brands, an agent should be careful not to link his client's
marketing viability with his athletic success. Rather, player representatives should pursue marketing strategies that transcend their
client's on-field performance. By focusing on characteristics besides
(or in addition to) the player's athletic performance, an agent can
extend the marketing life of a client well beyond his retirement.

Perhaps no player-agent pair has been more successful at
establishing such a long-term marketing strategy than legendary
golfer Arnold Palmer and the one-time head of IMG, Mark McCormack. Often credited as the pioneers of athlete endorsements,
Palmer and McCormack enjoyed unprecedented marketing success
by engaging in strategies that went beyond Palmer's performance
on the golf course. As Palmer himself states, "A brilliant part of
Mark's marketing strategy was never to tie my endorsement of a
product to how I was faring on the golf course. 'Win ads' were
about winning or losing, and his aim was never to position me as a
'winner' because there always comes a day when a winner no
longer wins. Then his appeal, accordingly, dramatically dips." By
focusing on Palmer's human qualities—his charm, his integrity, his
reliability—the popularity of Palmer's brand has endured long after
he stopped competing on the golf course.[99]

A more contemporary example involves pro skateboarder Tony
Hawk. Similar to Palmer, Hawk and his agent created a brand
around his name that has persisted well past his retirement. In
Hawk's case, his agent was able to transform his intangible assets—his well-known name, his reputation as an elite skateboarder,
his "cool" image—into a variety of tangible assets that continue to
generate revenue. Indeed, through self-named video games, book
deals, movie appearances, television production deals and a line of
skateboarding products, Hawk has been able to transcend the
skateboarding market and appeal to a variety of young people who
have never placed a foot on a skateboard.

Not every athlete will be successful enough to generate his own
brand, and agents must seek out different opportunities for those
clients. Many former athletes (such as Charles Barkley and Joe
Morgan), go into broadcasting, along with a host of far less famous
names. Agents should gauge their maturing clients' interest in such
opportunities, make contacts with networks early, and ensure that
any athlete interested in broadcasting cultivates good relationships
with the media and develops his skills as a commentator.

99. Today, Palmer holds eight licenses for his swimwear, golf accessories,
footwear, towels and handkerchiefs, he-
adwear, stationary, eyewear, small leath-
er goods and umbrellas which are sold
all over American and even as far off as
Japan.

Additionally, post-career opportunities vary from sport to sport. Some athletes may be interested in coaching, acting, or licensing their names and likenesses for use in the restaurant business. Many retired golfers sign lucrative deals to design golf courses. Pro-active planning—even during the peak stages of an athlete's career—will maximize the options available.

From start to finish, the agent plays a critical role in building his client's image and long-term marketing success. While the athlete's talent is what initially attracts endorsements, it is the agent who serves as the liaison between the player and the companies. The agent must not only maintain the health of those relationships, but must also use those endorsements to expand into other markets and demographics. The agent must be able to identify what makes his client unique and seek endorsements and marketing opportunities to promote that image. Finally, the agent must be able to evolve through all the phases of his client's career, including retirement. As athletes change, so changes their marketability, and the most successful agents are those who are able to strategically manage their clients' assets throughout the entirety of their careers.

Chapter 5, Section A—Questions for Discussion

1. In today's sports world, what strategies should superstar athletes like Tiger Woods, Lebron James, or even Maria Sharapova use to "transcend" their sport? Or have they already done so? If so, how? If you were their agent, what marketing strategies would you employ now to secure their long-term marketing success?

2. In addition to identifying endorsements for clients at the end of their career, players may need assistance not only to identify endorsements at the end of their careers, but also to find new employment upon their retirements. For the more talented, recognizable players, the transition from athlete stardom to retirement is relatively smooth. Their on-field performance will generate a variety of post-career options as coaches, general managers, and for characters like Charley Barkley or John McEnroe, lucrative careers as sports commentators. Most professional athletes, however, do not enjoy these opportunities. Many are without college degrees, have not saved a large portion of their earnings, and are in need of sound career and financial advice.

3. What role do you think an agent should play at the retirement phase of a client's career? Should the agent be actively involved in seeking non-athletic career opportuni-

ties? Or is it better to begin looking for the new "younger player" once your current client is no longer income-producing? What would be the costs and benefits of each approach?

Negotiating on Behalf of the Mature Athlete

The Hypothetical "Major"

Consider the following "hypothetical", either assuming the role of the attorney of a former tennis champion ("champion") or of the Chief Legal Officer of the "Major" Tennis Championship ("Major" or "Championships").

Former Champion's Attorney

You are the attorney/agent for a mid–30's professional tennis player who previously won one of the four "major" tennis championships, ("the Major" or "the Championship.") Your client has been down on his luck for the past few years, and his ranking has since slipped below Top 50. You are trying to identify new sources of income for him, in order to retain him as a client and to attract new clients who will see what you can do for a former champion in his "sunset years."

As you are watching the current year's Championship (your client went out in an early round, before national television coverage began), you notice a "promotional commercial" for the Major in which your client's name, image, and likeness appear as part of a "collage" of former champions celebrating their prior Major championship.

In particular, you realize that the file footage that has been used not only shows your client winning a previous championship, but also shows him "celebrating" for one to two seconds in front of a courtside clock sponsored by Timex. Under the Timex clock, the following legend appears: "the official timing device of the Major Championships."[100]

You also notice that at the end of the commercial, the tournament promotes not only itself, but also one of its primary corporate sponsors, Timex, as a "proud sponsor" of the tournament. At the same time at the end of the commercial, the logo of Timex appears next to the logo of the tournament for two to three seconds.

---

100. As part of your client's "cele-bration," assume (hypothetically) that he threw his racket into the crowd (against the Major's Player–Entry Form rules). The racket then broke a fan's nose during the ensuing "fight" over possession of the racket in the crowd.

The fan's "joint and several liability" (hypothetical) tort lawsuit against the Major and the prior Champion is still pending and should also be resolved in the context of this negotiation via a "mutual release" agreement.

You contact the Chief Legal Officer of the tournament and tell him that you believe that such a use of your client's file footage is not permitted by the Major's Player Entry Form. You inform him that you want your client compensated for this use. You also tell him that you want the Player Entry Form amended for future use to protect against such "implied product endorsement" use, or else you will seek to file a class action on behalf of your client and all other tennis players whose file footage appeared in similar commercials where players' "publicity rights" were (allegedly) violated.

Key points to consider in the negotiation with the Major Chief Legal Officer include the following: (1) what is a "permissible use" of the tournament's file footage; (2) how should the Player Entry Form be amended; (3) how much should your client be compensated for the past use of the footage; (4) what "publicity rights" have been "misappropriated" by the Major in this commercial, and what product "categories" have been negatively impacted thereby. (Here, you can assume that the former Champion has a (low-end) multi-year endorsement agreement with Disney to wear the Mickey Mouse watch brand when competing in non-major (or other "public") tennis events.); (5) should you contact other players whose images were similarly used?

Keeping these questions in mind and referring to the Major Player Entry Form in the Teacher's Manual, how would you draft a new, "client-friendly" paragraph to clarify which rights (are being assigned to the Major by the player)?

The Major Tennis Championships' CLO

You are the Chief Legal Officer of one of the four "major" tennis championships, ("the Major"). Specifically, you advise the CEO and COO of the tournament regarding the text of the (time-honored) Player Entry Form.

In prior years, you have advised your clients that it is legally permissible to use file footage taken during the tournament to "promote" the tournament in television commercials. Now, one of your primary tournament sponsors ("Timex"—"the official timing device of the Championship") has asked that you end your commercial with a reference to its company as "one of the proud sponsors" of the tournament. Timex also wants its name and logo to appear next to the name of the tournament, as the commercial fades out for two to three seconds.

The Player Entry Form for the tournament arguably permits the use of all players' names, images, and likenesses for the purposes of "promoting" the tournament. Your clients have asked you to review the form to make sure it permits the above described use. You give them an unqualified "yes," and the commercial is filmed and televised.

After the airing of the commercial, the former Champion's attorney gets wind of the fact that you used footage of his client's Championship win in connection with the commercial promoting both the tournament and (arguably) Timex. This attorney now wants to renegotiate the Player Entry Form's terms to preclude such use, because you did not obtain his client's prior written permission for such a use. The attorney wants his client to be compensated for the use of the file footage. (See: "Hypothetical" facts provided to former Champion's attorney, *supra.*)

Key points to consider in the negotiation with the player's attorney include the following: (1) how to define "permissible uses" of the player's name, image, and likeness for the purpose of "promoting" the tournament; (2) whether to compensate any player whose file footage is used in connection with a Major sponsor's name/product (if so, how much?); (3) whether to preclude the player from participating in the tournament unless he agrees to abide by the Major's broad definition of the "permissible uses"; and (4) whether or not to amend (or rewrite?) the Player Entry Form in future years, to avoid such challenges in the future.

Keeping these questions in mind and referring to the Major Player Entry Form, as the Major's CLO, how would you draft a new, "client-friendly" Entry Form on behalf of the Major?

As usual, "exemplar" responses are set forth in the Teacher's Manual.

B. *Workers' Compensation for Athletes*

While the previous section has explored different strategies for maximizing a player's marketability at the end of a career that ends naturally, the following sections will examine the role of the player representative when a client's career is cut short through injury, or in some cases, where the athlete's career was never given a chance to start at all.

Workers' compensation programs provide compensation to employees who suffer accidental injury in the course of employment, regardless of whether anyone was at fault. Workers' compensation programs are paid for by the employer and generally provide medical treatment, physical and vocational rehabilitation, and earnings tied to the average wage of the state. Importantly, workers' compensation is the exclusive remedy for the employee, which means the employee cannot also bring a tort suit against the employer. For this reason, a number of professional athletes actually oppose workers' compensation programs. On the other hand, the benefits are crucial for many college athletes injured on the field. The following cases demonstrate the various ways these legal claims operate in college and professional sports.

College Athletes

For college athletes, the primary question is whether injured college athletes are "employees" for purposes of workers' compensation benefits. In other words, are the athletes receiving paid scholarships as rewards for their athletic prowess? Or are the scholarships "paid consideration" for their athletic services? The cases below help provide an answer to these questions.

- Edward Gary Van Horn was killed in a plane crash while flying home with his team from a football game. Van Horn's widow and children filed for death benefits under California's Workmen's Compensation Act claiming that the Van Horn had received an athletic scholarship and a job, and therefore was an employee of the University. In ruling for Van Horn's widow and children, the court noted that the evidence clearly indicated that Van Horn received his job and scholarship in return for his athletic participation. While there was no explicit contract, the court noted that it must "look through the form to determine whether consideration has been paid for services." As such, Van Horn was found to be an "employee" under the California statute. *Van Horn v. Industrial Acci. Com.*, 219 Cal. App. 2d 457 (Cal. App. 2d Dist. 1963).

- Ray Herbert Dennison was fatally injured in a college football game, and his widow sought compensation under the Worker Compensation Statute of Colorado. Dennison was a scholarship athlete and his widow argued that Dennison qualified as an "employee" under the statute. The court found that there was insufficient evidence to establish that he was under contract to play football for the college and denied her claim. *State Compensation Insurance Fund. v. Industrial Comm.*, 314 P.2d 288 (Colo. 1957).

  Compare this result to another Colorado Supreme Court case where the court found that a player could be compensated under the Colorado Worker Compensation Statute for injuries he suffered during practice. The student was also a paid employee of the university, and there was evidence of a contract that required the college to employ him as manager of the tennis courts so long as he played football. There, the court held that the student's employment was contingent on his football participation, and thus his injuries were an "incident" of his employment. *University of Denver v. Nemeth*, 257 P.2d 423 (Colo. 1953)

- Fred Rensing was a varsity football player at Indiana State University on a full scholarship that included free tuition, fees, room and board, books, tutoring and a limited number of game tickets. This scholarship could be renewed each year so long as he "actively participated in football competition." During a spring practice, Rensing sustained an injury that rendered him a quadriplegic. Shortly thereafter, Rensing sought workers' compensation benefits as an employee of the university.

The Fourth District rejected the University's argument that Rensing was not an employee because the scholarship was a gift intended to further the young man's education. Relying heavily on the cases cited above, the court held "Rensing and the Trustees of the Indiana University bargained for an exchange in the manner of employer and employee of Rensing's football talents for certain scholarship benefits." The court also noted that the trustees retained the right to terminate the agreement, which tended to point toward an employer-employee relationship. *Rensing v. Indiana State Univ.*, 437 N.E. 2d 78 (4th Cir. 1982)

The Supreme Court of Indiana, however, soundly rejected the Fourth Circuit's reasoning supporting the holding that scholarship athletes like Rensing or any other scholarship recipient "received benefits based upon their past demonstrated ability in various areas to enable them to pursue opportunities for higher education as well as to further progress in their own fields of endeavor." The Indiana Supreme Court went on to hold that there was no intent to enter into an employee-employer relationship, that Rensing's scholarship did not constitute "pay" under the statute and that the employer's right to discharge on the basis of performance (not participation) was also missing. As a result, Rensing was held to be a student-athlete and not an employee under Indiana's Workmen's Compensation Act. *Rensing v. Indiana State Univ.*, 444 N.E. 2d 1170 (Ind. 1983).

As these cases demonstrate, courts have struggled to define exactly what should be considered an employment relationship in the context of college sports. In a case shortly after *Rensing*, the Michigan Court of Appeals attempted to outline four relevant factors for the employee/student-athlete inquiry:

(1) The proposed employer's right to control or dictate the activities of the proposed employees;

(2) The proposed employer's right to discipline or fire the proposed employee;

    (3) The payment of "wages," and particularly, the extent to which the proposed employee is dependent upon the payment of wages or other benefits for his daily living expenses; and

    (4) Whether the task performed by the proposed employee was "an integral" part of the proposed employer's business.[101]

Would the above cases come out differently applying these four factors? How should they come out?

Professional Athletes

    Professional athletes can also bring workers' compensation claims as employees of their respective clubs. Unlike college athletes, there is no issue as to whether the athletes are employees. Nevertheless, a variety of questions do arise when applying workers' compensation statutes to physically demanding sports such as football. What sorts of injuries are "accidents"? What activities are considered "incident to employment"? Is off-season training part of the job? What if the athlete uses methods of training not approved by the club? The following cases address some of these issues.

- Gery Palmer suffered an injury while playing offensive guard for the Kansas City Chiefs. According to Palmer, the job of the offensive guard is to drive the opposing tackle out of position to create a hole for the running back. In describing the play in which he was injured, Palmer explained, "I just was actually off balance and had not had the opportunity to make the play work right for me."

        The legal issue stemmed from Missouri's workers' compensation statute, which grants compensation only if the claimant has established that the injury was the result of an accident and not from stresses usually incident to the work performance. Missouri's Industrial Commission found that Palmer's injury was the result of an "abnormal strain," which is treated as an "accident" under the statute. An abnormal strain is characterized as work done in an awkward or unbalanced posture that produces an excessive strain, despite being the performance of a normal duty. Finding that Palmer's injury resulted from performing a usual occupation in an unusual manner, the Industrial Commission granted relief.

        On appeal, the Court of Appeals of Missouri overturned the Commission, finding that there was nothing distinct about this particular instance. Palmer was simply

101. *Coleman v. Western Michigan University*, 125 Mich. App. 35 (1983).

bested by his defensive opponent, a common occurrence in the course of a standard football game. Rather than an "abnormal strain," the injury was an "expected incident of the usual work task done in the usual way." On these grounds, the Court denied relief to Palmer. *Palmer v. Kansas City Chiefs*, 621 S.W.2d 350 (Mo. App. 1981).

• Eric Dandenault, a professional hockey player for the Philadelphia Flyers, suffered injuries to his abdomen and groin while playing hockey in the off-season to stay in shape. Dandenault admitted that he did not have the approval of the team to play (as required by his contract), but contended that all professional hockey players participated in summer leagues, that the teams knew players did so, and that it was a necessary step to stay in shape for the upcoming season. Nonetheless, the court held that the team neither gave permission nor encouraged Dandenault to participate in summer leagues. Thus, his injury did not arise "in the course of employment," and his claim was denied. *Dandenault v. W.C.A.B. (Philadelphia Flyers)*, 728 A.2d 1001 (Pa. Cmwlth. Ct. 1999).

• NFL player Paul Farren was injured while training in the off-season and applied for relief under the workers' compensation statute. His team, the Baltimore Ravens, argued that Farren was not under contract at the time of the injury and thus was not an employee.

Reversing the lower court, the Court of Appeals of Ohio held that Farren met the statutory requirements of an employee. While recognizing that Farren was not under an explicit, written contract, it noted that off-season conditioning was a necessary task to perform at the professional level. The Court also recognized that Farren believed off-season training was mandatory and that he was told that his position was a year-round job. It finally concluded that there was enough evidence to reasonably conclude that Farren was encouraged or directed to train in the off-season. *Farren v. Baltimore Ravens, Inc.*, 130 Ohio App.3d 533 (1998).

Can these last two cases be reconciled? Unlike Farren, Dandenault was under contract at the time of his injury, but the court remained unwilling to consider his off-season training part of his employment. More broadly, can a team reasonably expect a player *not* to perform off-season conditioning?

In principle, workers' compensation aims to provide a sure and speedy method for employees to obtain compensation without having to prove fault on the part of their employer. However, the

modest compensation amounts and the exclusivity of the relief have
caused many players to seek remedies outside the workers' compensation statutes. While courts still generally recognize professional
athletes as "employees" under the statute, they have also developed a number of legal doctrines to limit the exclusivity of workers
compensation and to allow certain tort claims to proceed.

Limitations to Workers' Compensation

When athletes are injured and receive workers' compensation,
they sometimes try to recover additional monies through the civil
justice system, such as when they feel they were intentionally
defrauded by their employer to their detriment. Such was the case
with William Gambrell.

Gambrell was drafted by the Kansas City Chiefs in 1974.
Before participating in any games, Gambrell was examined by the
team physicians and found to be fit to play. Unfortunately, in a preseason game, Gambrell permanently injured his back and neck
forcing him to retire. He filed for and was awarded workers'
compensation benefits in the amount of $5,250 paid for by the
Chiefs. Soon after, he filed an additional multi-million dollar lawsuit alleging fraud and deceit by the Chiefs and the team doctors.
Specifically, he claimed the doctors knew, or should have known, of
his pre-existing disability and that they intentionally concealed the
disability to ensure Gambrell would continue to play for the Chiefs.

On appeal, the court separated injuries involving fraud or
deceit into two categories: "those in which the deceit follows the
injury and produces a second injury or loss." Those injuries in the
first category are generally barred from further tort actions because
the deceit has "merged" into the injury for which the employee
already received compensation. Those in the second category are
found to be separate and distinct injuries that are not precluded by
workers' compensation statutes.

In the end, the court found that Gambrell's injuries were of the
first category: "No matter how his cause of action is framed, his
claim ultimately reduces to one for bodily injuries for which compensation can be and actually has been had by plaintiff under the
Workmen's Compensation Act." *Gambrell v. Kansas City Chiefs*,
562 S.W.2d 163 (Mo. App. 1978)

Does this categorization adopted by the court make sense? Is it
fair to the athlete? Is it fair that Gambrell's legal remedies are the
same as an injured athlete who was not misled or deceived about
his fitness going into a football game?

Uncertainty in Calculating Damages & the Rise of Collec-
tively-Bargained Solutions

Given the brevity of the average athlete's career—which we
discussed in Section A of this chapter—courts have struggled with

calculating just how much injured players have lost in wages due to injuries. How do courts determine how long a player would have played? The uncertainty was problematic for courts and franchise owners, who were afraid that they would be forced to pay exceedingly large workers' compensation payments to injured players. This, in turn, led predictably to collectively-bargained solutions.

In 1977, the Chicago Bears picked Ted Albrecht in the first round of the draft. After five successful seasons, Albrecht suffered a back injury that ended his career. Shortly thereafter, he began running his own business and started working as a sportscaster earning an annual salary approximately $50,000 less than what he would have made as an NFL player.

Under the applicable statute, wage loss benefits are provided to those who had been "partially incapacitated from pursuing his usual and customary line of employment." The benefits included compensation for the duration of the disability, equal to two-thirds of the difference between what he made in his previous employment before he was injured, and what he makes after the accident. The Bears argued that these provisions could not be applied to NFL players because their careers were too short, and it was too speculative for a court to determine that it was a football injury that incapacitated the player. However, the Court of Appeals of Illinois rejected the Bears' argument, holding that football players were comparable to at-will employees. It further found that Albrecht had started every game for five years and there was sufficient evidence that he would have continued to do so but for his injury. As such, the court awarded wage loss benefits.[102] *Albrecht v. The Industrial Commission*, 271 Ill.App.3d 756 (1995)

After the case, NFL owners became increasingly concerned about workers' compensation benefits being applied to the high salaries and short careers of NFL players. In light of this concern, many owners tried to persuade state legislatures to cap the amount of financial benefits payable to injured players. Others focused on dealing with these issues through collective bargaining. But that path has also encountered substantial difficulty.

The Bert Bell NFL Retirement Plan is a collectively-bargained program that provides pension benefits for players in retirement. It also ensures that players who suffer from permanent disabilities receive a modest flow of income from current players. Specifically, the Bell Plan has two kinds of benefits for permanently disabled players: Level 1 benefits of $4,000 a month for players whose disability was due to "a football injury incurred while an Active

102. Importantly, the court found the base for calculating the wage differential to be Albrecht's 1982 salary, and not the increasing salaries of the years to follow.

Player," and Level 2 benefits of $1,800 a month if the total disability "resulted from other than a football injury."

In *Brumm v. Bert Bell NFL Retirement Plan*, Donald Brumm challenged the ruling that qualified him for only Level 2 benefits. As a ten-year veteran in the league, Brumm had accumulated a number of injuries to his back and knees during his career. When his career ended, he began work as a truck driver. After a traffic accident, however, Brumm soon found himself unable to work. In his physical examination after the accident, the physician noted that Brumm had a pre-existing condition that stemmed from his football experience.

Despite this medical report, the Bell Board and the District Court both determined Brumm's injuries entitled him to Level 2 benefits. Specifically, the District Court agreed with the Bell Board that "Level 1 benefits were payable only to a player who incurred his disability from *one* identifiable football injury." Furthermore, the player had to become totally and permanently disabled within a "reasonable amount of time after leaving football." Any player with injuries not meeting these requirements received only Level 2 benefits.

On appeal, the Eighth Circuit found such an interpretation to be clearly contrary to the purpose of the Plan. As the court noted, "If the Plan's goal is to take care of the players as part of their compensation for investing themselves in the sport, players who suffer a series of football injuries resulting in disability are as entitled to consideration as those suffering a single disabling injury." *Brumm v. Bert Bell NFL Retirement Plan*, 995 F.2d 1433 (8th Cir. 1993). The questions that resulted from this case generally asked how far this protection should extend and under what circumstances. For example, former San Diego Chargers offensive guard Walter Sweeney challenged his denial of Level 1 benefits by claiming his addiction to drugs and alcohol after his career had stemmed from his use of amphetamines, barbiturates and anabolic steroids that were prescribed by team doctors.[103] When the district court ruled in Sweeney's favor, the NFLPA immediately appealed, fearing an onslaught of similar drug-addiction based disability claims that would have to be paid out of the NFLPA's pocket. However, the Sweeney holding was ultimately reversed by the Ninth Circuit, and, since that time, courts have consistently held that drug-addiction or mental anguish type disabilities do not qualify for Level 1 benefits.

103. *Sweeney v. Bert Bell NFL Player Retirement Plan*, 961 F. Supp. 1381 (S.D.Cal. 1997).

Tort Claims for Athletes

As mentioned earlier, courts have recognized certain limitations to the exclusivity of workers' compensation statutes. The next section will take a closer look at three common tort claims in the world of sports: medical malpractice, defective products and hazardous facilities.

Medical Malpractice

Today, courts are increasingly recognizing tort claims against employers for the intentional infliction of physical injury. In the context of professional sports, this includes the deliberate concealment of an athlete's medical information by the team physicians.

In *Krueger v. San Francisco Forty Niners*, 189 Cal.App.3d 823 (1987), the 49ers team doctor consistently chose not to tell All–Pro tackle, Charlie Krueger, about the long-term health issues he faced from a series of knee injuries and operations he had experienced during his career. The Court held that the intentional failure to disclose foreseeable risks stemming from previous injuries constituted the tort of fraudulent concealment, especially because the concealment was done with the deliberate purpose of inducing the professional athlete to keep playing. Shortly after the decision, Krueger settled with the 49ers for $1 million.

How does this result compare to the *Gambrell* case discussed above? What facts, if any, explain the difference in the outcomes?

Another issue that courts have faced is whether team doctors are "employees" of the team (and protected by workers' compensation exclusivity) or independent contractors liable for potential tort claims. *Bryant v. Fox & Chicago Bears*, 162 Ill.App.3d 46 (1987) illustrates this dilemma. Two Chicago Bears football players brought a medical malpractice action against an orthopedic surgeon used by the team. The Bears argued that the doctor was an employee of the team, and as a result, the players' relief was limited to their workers' compensation claims. By contrast, the players argued that the surgeon was not an employee, but rather an independent contractor.

To make this determination, the Court looked to a number of factors: the right to control the manner in which the work is done; method of payment; right to discharge; skill required; who provides tools, materials, or equipment; whether the workmen's occupation is related to that of the alleged employer; and whether the alleged employer deducted for withholding tax." The Court went on to note that the right to control the manner in which the work was done was the single most important factor.

Applying these facts to the case at hand, the Court found there to be insufficient evidence to support the lower court's finding that the doctor was an employee. The team had little control over the doctor's actions, he billed the Bears separately for each surgery, he used equipment that belonged to a hospital, the Bears did not provide him with W–2 forms and the doctor received no benefits, insurance or pension from the team. For these reasons, the Court found that the evidence did not demonstrate that the team had sufficient control over the doctor's professional activities to establish that he was an "employee" and therefore, granted the Bears' motion for dismissal. *Bryant v. Fox & Chicago Bears*, 162 Ill.App.3d 46 (1987).

In light of this suit and a host of others brought by players against team doctors, many malpractice insurers are hesitant to provide coverage for doctors whose patients are professional athletes. Others have continued to provide coverage, but only after requiring that the team physicians sign explicit employment contracts with their clubs.

Defective Products

Another common target for injured athletes is the manufacturer of the equipment used in competition. The most targeted equipment of all: the helmet. For example, Kevin Byrns suffered an injury to his head after being hit in a head-to-head collision during an on-side kick in a high school varsity football game. Seeking relief for his injuries, Byrns sued the manufacturer of his helmet. The Arizona Supreme Court required that the plaintiff prove that a defect made the defendant's product "unreasonably dangerous." To determine whether a product poses unreasonable danger, the court declared the test to be "whether a reasonable manufacturer would continue to market his product in the same condition as he sold it to the plaintiff with knowledge of the potential dangerous consequences the trial just revealed."

Building on this test, the court adopted a seven-factor analysis to determine if a defect is unreasonably dangerous: (1) the usefulness and desirability of the product, (2) the availability of other and safer products to meet the same need, (3) the likelihood of injury and its probable seriousness, (4) the obviousness of the danger, (5) common knowledge and normal public expectations of the danger (particularly for established products), (6) the avoidability of injury by care in use of the product (including the effect of instructions and warnings), and (7) the ability to eliminate the danger without seriously impairing the usefulness of the product or making it unduly expensive.

Applying these factors to Byrns' helmet, the court found the possibility of a sling defect that could cause a potentially dangerous "bottoming out" effect. It also held that questions of causation and place of impact were for the jury to decide and thus reversed the directed verdict for the manufacturer, Riddell. *Byrns v. Riddell*, 113 Ariz. 264 (1976). (In this context please consider the "crusade" to introduce more effective, anti-concussive helments which is being led by former Harvard College football star/WWF wrestler, Chris Nowinski. *See*: The Sports Legacy Institute, www.sportslegacy.org.)

Hazardous Facilities

Injured athletes can also file suit against owners of facilities for creating a hazardous condition that contributed to the player's injury. Elliot Maddox, a baseball player for the New York Yankees, was injured at Shea Stadium due to a wet spot in the outfield. While attempting to throw the ball in from the outfield, Maddox claimed that his left foot "took off" on the wet spot while his right foot remained stuck in a puddle, causing injury. Maddox admitted to previously noticing the standing water and also admitted that he had played on wet fields before. He also admitted that he never requested to be substituted for by a replacement.

The legal issue facing Maddox was whether his claim was barred due to the "assumption of risk" doctrine. Courts have generally held that athletes competing in games and events assume the risks of injury that are normally associated with the sport. In response, Maddox argued that: (1) employers have a statutory obligation to provide a safe place to work and (2) that continuation of a dangerous job after being directed by a superior to proceed does not constitute assumption of the risk. The Court however rejected both of Maddox's claims, holding first that Maddox did not qualify for the statute guaranteeing a safe workplace, and even if he did, he failed to show any fault on the part of his employer. Secondly, the Court found no evidence to support Maddox's contention that he was directed to take the field despite the danger. Had he informed the manager of the dangerous conditions and still been ordered to play, the Court conceded the result might be different. Here, however, Maddox merely commented to the manager that the field was wet, and the only person that Maddox actually informed of the conditions was an unidentified grounds crew member. For these reasons, summary dismissal against Maddox was granted.

Is the Court's reasoning compelling? Should assumption of risk be a valid defense to an athlete's hazardous facilities claims? For what types of hazards can it be said that a baseball player did not assume the risk?

C. *Disability and the Right to Play*

While the previous cases have discussed the legal remedies for players whose careers were cut short due to past injuries, the following section will examine the legal justifications used to prohibit athletes from participating in order to prevent future injuries and the resulting liabilities.

One of the most famous disability cases was brought by Nicholas Knapp. Knapp received a scholarship to play basketball at Northwestern University. However, before he began school, he suffered sudden cardiac failure during a high school basketball game. Knapp recovered, but his heart condition remained. As a result, Northwestern disqualified him from playing for its basketball team (while still honoring his scholarship). In response, Knapp filed suit under the Rehabilitation Act of 1973.

To prevail on his claim for discrimination under the Rehabilitation Act of 1973, Knapp had to establish four key factors: (1) he was "disabled" as defined by the act; (2) he was otherwise qualified for the position sought; (3) he was excluded from the position solely because of his disability; and (4) the position existed as part of a program or activity receiving federal financial assistance.

To be "disabled" under the act, Knapp had to prove that one or more major life activities (i.e. caring for one's self, performing manual tasks, walking, seeing, hearing, speaking, breathing, learning, and working) was substantially impaired by his physical disability. Although Knapp tried to argue that playing college basketball was an integral part of his major life activity of learning, the Court rejected his particularized definition of "major life activity." As the Court noted, an exclusion from playing intercollegiate sports does not mean a student cannot learn. Additionally, the Court found Knapp was not "otherwise qualified" because his condition still posed a reasonable probability of substantial harm. Finally, the Court held that where its decisions are based on credible evidence, a university should be given the right to determine its acceptable levels of risk. *Knapp v. Northwestern Univ.*, 101 F.3d 473 (7th Cir. 1996).

Another issue that has arisen among public schools is the practice of requiring all students participating in school athletics to sign a waiver releasing the school of all liability. Several school districts in Washington adopted a policy requiring all students seeking participation in interscholastic athletics to sign a generic type of a blanket release that absolved the district from "liability resulting from ordinary negligence that may arise in connection with the school district's interscholastic activities programs."

In evaluating whether such a release should be deemed invalid for violating public policy, the Court looked to six factors that generally indicate when such a release of liability is contrary to public policy: (1) the agreement concerns an endeavor of a type generally thought suitable for public regulation; (2) the party seeking exculpation is engaged in performing a service of great importance to the public, which is often a matter of practical necessity for some members of the public; (3) such party holds itself out as willing to perform this service for any member of the public who seeks it, or at least for any member coming within certain established standards; (4) because of the essential nature of the service, in the economic setting of the transition, the party invoking exculpation possesses a decisive advantage of bargaining strength against any member of the public who seeks the services; (5) in exercising a superior bargaining power, the party confronts the public with a standardized adhesion contract of exculpation, and makes no provision whereby a purchaser may pay additional reasonable fees and obtain protection against negligence; and (6) the person or property of members of the public seeking such services must be placed under the control of the furnisher of the services, subject to the risk of carelessness on the part of the furnisher, its employees or agents. Applying these factors, the court found all six factors were present, and thus the releases were invalid as against public policy. *Wagenblast v. Odessa School District*, 110 Wash.2d 845 (1988).

In *Odessa*, the court focused on the public nature of high school sports. Would its reasoning apply to college sports? Professional sports? Please consider constructing additional "interactive hypothetical" to probe the responses to these and the other questions raised in Sections B and C of this chapter.

Chapter 6

THE LEGAL RELATIONSHIP BETWEEN THE AGENCY AND ITS EMPLOYEES

In Chapter 1, we described the law governing agents and their representation of clients. In this chapter, the discussion turns to the employment relationship between sports agencies and their agents from the moment when a given agent first joins the firm through the time when the employment relationship is terminated, and the agent embarks on other career opportunities.

During the course of an agent's employment at a sports agency, the agent is likely to acquire knowledge, skills, and expertise in representing professional athletes. More important, the agent will develop personal relationships with the clients he represents and pursues on behalf of the agency. When the employment relationship between the agent and the firm ends, the agent will set out to pursue other career opportunities. As the agent becomes an actual or potential competitor with respect to his former employer, what restrictions exist on the agent's freedom to exploit the information and personal relationships acquired during the course of his employment?

From the agent's perspective, he would ideally like to draw upon the valuable experience gained during his time at the agency, while continuing to represent the clients he worked for on behalf of the firm. On the other hand, the agency's objective is likely to be to prohibit its former employee and future competitor from taking advantage of the firm's proprietary information, or, even worse, depriving the agency of clients. What can the agency do to protect its business from competition with a former agent?

This chapter is divided into two parts. The first describes the background law governing the relationship between employers and employees. It also discusses the protective measures, including

124

incorporating covenants not to compete into the standard employment agreement, that an agency can take at the outset of the employment relationship as the agent enters the agency. The second part addresses the legal recourse available to the firm after the agent has left when the agency learns that its former employee has breached it duties, including restrictions under the non-competition agreement.

PART I: THE AGENT ENTERING THE MEGA– AGENCY

Both during the course of employment and even afterwards, several bodies of law strike the balance between the employee's freedom to pursue other career opportunities and the employer's ability to protect its business. This section will outline: (1) the common law duty of loyalty, which bars an employee from competing with his current employer; (2) trade secret protections, in the form of statutory prohibitions against misappropriation of trade secrets and the inevitable disclosure doctrine, which prevents an employee from disclosing his former employee's trade secrets even in the absence of misappropriation; and (3) covenants not to compete, which are contractual agreements between an employer and employee that restrict the employee's activities following the termination of his employment.

The discussion of each of these areas will highlight the fact that when the employer is a sports agency, the degree to which these legal doctrines can protect the employer's interests varies significantly. Although the duty of loyalty restricts an agent from beginning to compete with the agency while he is still employed at the firm, this protection ceases once the employment is terminated. Trade secret law may safeguard valuable agency information, such as client lists. However, the preponderance of the agency's most precious assets, including the firm's relationships with its clients, do not classify as trade secrets and are not protected under this body of law. Therefore, in order to secure its interests, an agency will have to rely heavily upon covenants not to compete. While the restrictions that can be included in these agreements are limited, these provisions are the agency's best means of protecting its business from the threat of competition from a former employee.

A. The Duty of Loyalty

Employees are bound to observe a duty of loyalty to their employers during the term of employment. The Restatement of Agency explains the limitations this duty imposes upon the employee's liberty to compete with his employer:

> Throughout the duration of an agency relationship, an agent has a duty to refrain from competing with the principal and

from taking action on behalf of or otherwise assisting the principal's competitors. During that time, an agent may take action, not otherwise wrongful, to prepare for competition following termination of the agency relationship.[104]

In the jurisdictions where this general rule applies (such as Ohio), the agency will be safeguarded from competition on behalf of its agents during their terms of employment.[105] Of particular importance to the sports agency is the fact that during the course of the employment relationship, an employee cannot solicit clients away from the firm in preparation for future competition.[106]

However, the protection the duty of loyalty offers to the agency is clearly limited by the fact that the duty expires upon the agent's exodus from the firm. Furthermore, during the term of employment, the agent remains free to prepare for competition against the agency. An agent can plan to join a competitor or lay the groundwork for his own competing agency, then immediately solicit business from his agency clients upon exiting the firm. For the agency, this possibility highlights the relative weakness of the protections offered by the duty of loyalty. Another important consideration for the agency is that even if the firm can prove that an employee has breached the duty of loyalty, a court may award monetary damages, but is unlikely to order an injunction to prevent solicitation of the agency's clients.[107]

B.   Trade Secret Protection

Employers can invoke trade secret law to safeguard proprietary information that can be classified as a "trade secret." This section will outline: (1) statutory protections of trade secrets, which prohibit an employee from misappropriating the employer's trade secrets; and (2) the inevitable disclosure doctrine, which prevents employ-

---

104. RESTATEMENT (THIRD) OF AGENCY § 8.04 (2007).

105. Note that the Restatement's rule is similar to Ohio law. In Ohio, courts have concluded that an employee "owes his or her employer a duty to act 'in the utmost good faith and loyalty toward his ... employer.'" *Berge v. Columbus Community Cable Access*, 736 N.E.2d 517, 549 (Ohio Ct. App. 1999) (quoting *Connelly v. Balkwill*, 116 N.E.2d 701, 707 (Ohio 1954)). An employee also has the right to prepare for future competition with an employer provided that this planning is not done during work hours and that the competition does not begin until after the relationship is terminated. *Michael Shore & Co. v. Greenwald*, 1985 WL 17713, at *2 (Ohio Ct. App. March 21, 1985).

106. RESTATEMENT (THIRD) OF AGENCY § 8.04 cmt. c (2007).

107. This proposition is consistent with Ohio law. *See Extracorporeal Alliance, L.L.C. v. Rosteck*, 285 F.Supp.2d 1028, 1044 (N.D. Ohio 2003) (finding that even though it was "substantially likely" that a plaintiff would prevail on a breach of the duty of loyalty claim against a former employee, injunctive relief would not be granted because any injury would be fully compensable by monetary damages and therefore not irreparable). *See also Basicomputer Corp. v. Scott*, 973 F.2d 507, 511 (6th Cir. 1992) (stating that harm is "not irreparable if it is fully compensable by monetary damages").

ees who have acquired knowledge of their employers' trade secrets from accepting employment with a competitor, even in the absence of misappropriation. Our analysis will then shift to the perspective of the sports agency, revealing that trade secret law may prove useful in a limited context. However, because the most valuable resources an agent has access to while employed at the agency, including personal relationships with clients, do not classify as "trade secrets," the agency cannot rely upon this body of law to fully preserve its business interests.

1. Statutory Protection Against Trade Secret Misappropriation

The Uniform Trade Secrets Act offers a broad definition of the information that can receive trade secret protection.[108] The Act states that:

"Trade secret" means information, including a formula, pattern, compilation, program, device, method, technique, or process, that:

(i) derives independent economic value, actual or potential, from not being generally known to, and not being readily ascertainable by proper means by, other persons who can obtain economic value from its disclosure or use, and

(ii) is the subject of efforts that are reasonable under the circumstances to maintain its secrecy.[109]

In the event that an employer's trade secrets are actually misappropriated,[110] or there is a threat that this information will be misappropriated, the Act offers injunctive relief.[111] Monetary dam-

---

108. The vast majority of states, including Ohio, have adopted statutes based upon the Uniform Trade Secrets Act.

109. UNIF. TRADE SECRETS ACT § 1(4) (1985).

110. The Act defines "misappropriation" as:

(i) acquisition of a trade secret of another by a person who knows or has reason to know that the trade secret was acquired by improper means; or

(ii) disclosure or use of a trade secret of another without express or implied consent by a person who

(A) used improper means to acquire knowledge of the trade secret; or

(B) at the time of disclosure or use, knew or had reason to know that his knowledge of the trade secret was

(I) derived from or through a person who had utilized improper means to acquire it;

(II) acquired under circumstances giving rise to a duty to maintain its secrecy or limit its use; or

(III) derived from or through a person who owed a duty to the person seeking relief to maintain its secrecy or limit its use; or

(C) before a material change of his [or her] position, knew or had reason to know that it was a trade secret and that knowledge of it had been acquired by accident or mistake. *Id.* at § 1(2).

"Improper means" includes theft, bribery, misrepresentation, breach or inducement of a breach of a duty to maintain secrecy, or espionage through electronic or other means. *Id.* at § 1(1).

111. *Id.* at § 2(a).

ages, including the actual loss and unjust enrichment, caused by the misappropriation are also available under the Act.[112]

Even in the absence of misappropriation, a judicially created doctrine called "inevitable disclosure" may serve to prevent former employees from utilizing an employer's trade secrets.

2. The Inevitable Disclosure Doctrine

In the absence of actual or threatened misappropriation of trade secrets, the inevitable disclosure doctrine empowers courts to enjoin an employee from accepting a new position in which he will "inevitably disclose" his former employer's trade secrets.[113] Therefore, in the jurisdictions that have adopted this doctrine, courts will essentially draft a non-competition agreement limiting the positions a former employee can assume.[114]

The inevitable disclosure doctrine is another mechanism an employer can utilize to limit competition on the behalf of former employees. However, as with statutes prohibiting misappropriation, this doctrine is also limited to safeguarding trade secrets.

3. Limitations

Despite the remedies available by statute and the inevitable disclosure doctrine, it is unlikely that an agency will cure the problems of employee defection through trade secret protections. First, much of the valuable information an agent is likely to exploit, as well as the agent's relationships with clients, are not trade secrets. Secondly, the type of employer information that may classify as a trade secret is more likely to be generally known, and therefore unprotected, when the employer is a sports agency.

The fracturing of the mega-agency Steinberg Moorad & Dunn ("SMD") illustrates the limited effectiveness of trade secret protections that an agency can invoke against a former employee. When David Dunn attempted to end his partnership with Leigh Steinberg and Jeff Moorad to start his own competing agency, Athletes First, SMD filed suit alleging misappropriation of trade secrets, among other claims.[115] In reversing a judgment and award of damages exceeding $44 million against Dunn and Athletes First, the Ninth Circuit held that SMD's client list information was not a trade

---

112. *Id.* at § 3(a). If malicious or willful misappropriation occurs, exemplary damages not to exceed twice the amount described may also be awarded. *Id.* at § 3(b).

113. *See PepsiCo, Inc. v. Redmond,* 54 F.3d 1262, 1272 (7th Cir. 1995). Factors a court will consider include whether the former and prospective employers are competitors, the degree to which the employee's responsibilities in his former

and prospective employment overlap, and whether the prospective employer has made efforts to reduce the likelihood of disclosure. *Id.* at 1267.

114. Ohio has adopted the inevitable disclosure doctrine. *See Procter & Gamble v. Stoneham,* 747 N.E.2d 268, 274 (Ohio Ct. App. 2000).

115. *Steinberg Moorad & Dunn, Inc. v. Dunn,* 136 F.App'x 6 (9th Cir. 2005).

secret because it was available to all agents.[116] With regard to claims that Dunn utilized particular "player desires and preferences" to recruit athletes away from SMD, the court ruled that this information, which included one player's goals in securing marketing and endorsement deals and another athlete's hopes of becoming involved in entertainment, was not protected because it could not be demonstrated that these aspirations were not generally known.[117]

The fact that the agency's clients are well-known and subjected to media scrutiny can undermine the firm's ability to claim the protections of trade secrets. The clients' fame increases the probability that particular information about them will become public knowledge. Furthermore, sports leagues and their respective players associations impose regulations upon agents that force agencies to accept more transparency than other employers. For example, a typical employer can usually protect a list of clients as a trade secret.[118] However, an agency's client list might be readily available to the public. For example, in the case of SMD, the National Football League Players Association (NFLPA) had published a list of players and their representatives on its website.[119] Other data, including player salaries, is also public information.[120] In fact, during the SMD litigation, the NFLPA took the position that there was nothing secret about the information a sports agent needs to be successful.[121]

Trade secret law may still play a limited role in protecting an agency's information. For example, as the Ninth Circuit indicated in its review of SMD's lawsuit, confidential information such as a player's unhappiness with his current team and his desire to sign with another franchise can classify as a trade secret.[122] However, given athletes' high profiles and the constant media scrutiny they receive, it may prove difficult to prevent information about players, including their goals and preferences, from becoming generally known.

From the agency's point of view, the limitations of trade secret protection indicate the importance of contracting with an agent to guard against the employee's future competition with the firm.

116. *Id.* at 12.

117. *Id.* at 12–13.

118. Note that in Ohio, provided an employer takes reasonable steps to safeguard this information, trade secret protection extends even to those lists that a former employee can compile from memory alone. *See Al Minor & Assocs. v. Martin*, 881 N.E.2d 850, 851 (Ohio 2008).

119. *Steinberg Moorad & Dunn, Inc. v. Dunn*, 2002 WL 31968234, at *15 (C.D. Cal. Dec. 26, 2002).

120. *Id.*

121. *Id.* (citing the deposition of Richard Berthelsen, General Counsel of the NFLPA).

122. *Dunn*, 136 F.App'x at 12–13.

C. Non–Competition Agreements

From the perspective of the agency, the inclusion of a covenant not to compete within the firm's employment contracts with its agents is of paramount importance. Without these restraints, the agent may exploit any information acquired during his employment, provided it is not protected as a trade secret. Furthermore, the agent can solicit his former employer's clients and employees in an effort to lure them away from the agency.

As a result, sports agencies will typically incorporate these restrictive covenants into their contracts with agents. These agreements can include clauses that bar a former employee from: (1) soliciting the agency's clients, (2) participating in the hiring of other agency personnel, or (3) working on behalf of the agency's major competitors.

However, the extent to which an agency can restrict a departing agent's future employment opportunities is not unlimited. It should be noted that in the majority of jurisdictions, post-employment agreements not to compete are disfavored by the law because of their restraining effect on trade.[123] The following passage addresses the elements a court will consider in enforcing non-competition agreements.

1. The Enforceability of Non–Competition Agreements

An employer's ability to enforce covenants not to compete against a former employee varies widely across jurisdictions.[124] In general, a non-competition agreement is enforceable if it is: (1) ancillary to a valid contract, (2) reasonable, and (3) supported by adequate consideration.[125]

a. Ancillary to a Valid Contract

In general, a covenant is ancillary to an employment contract if it is secondary to the primary purpose of the employment.[126] In the case of the sports agency, it will almost certainly be the case that the restraints in a non-competition agreement with the agency's employees are ancillary to these employees' primary functions, namely recruiting and representing clients.

It should be noted that entering into a non-competition agreement after the employment term has started can be problematic.

---

123. 54A AM. JUR. 2D MONOPOLIES AND RESTRAINT OF TRADE § 888 (2008).

124. For example, in California, these restraints on trade are especially disfavored. See CAL. BUS. & PROF. CODE § 16600 (WEST 2008).

125. 36 CAUSES OF ACTION 2D 103 § 2 (2007)

126. Id. at § 3.

Nevertheless, provided that the later agreement is supported by independent consideration, it will likely be found enforceable.[127]

b. Reasonableness

Although standards vary across jurisdictions, a covenant not to compete will generally be enforced to the extent it is deemed "reasonable." A non-competition agreement is "reasonable" if: (1) its terms are no greater than necessary to protect the employer's legitimate interest, and (2) the employer's interest is not outweighed by undue harm to the employee and the likely injury to the public.[128]

The strength of the sports agency's legitimate interest in enforcing a covenant not to compete depends upon the particular circumstances and the jurisdiction. In states where customer relationships can be safeguarded, the employer's legitimate interest in imposing the covenant will be heightened.[129]

In evaluating the reasonableness of particular restraints, courts have described a plethora of factors to consider, but have tended to focus upon: (1) the time duration of the restraint, (2) its geographical area, (3) and the scope of the activity which is limited.[130] In terms of drafting an effective covenant, however, a sports agency may not want to rely upon conventional geographic limitations because the firm has a greater interest in preventing competition over particular clients.

Another approach to crafting restrictive covenants is to focus on preventing a former employee from competing through solicitation of the employer's clients. Although courts generally enforce restraints barring employees from recruiting business from their

---

127. *Id.*

128. *See* RESTATEMENT (SECOND) OF CONTRACTS § 188 (1981). Under Ohio law, courts look to the same elements to evaluate the "reasonableness" of a non-competition agreement. *See Raimonde v. van Vlerah*, 325 N.E.2d 544, 547 (Ohio 1975).

129. Ohio is a state where customer relationships are protected. *See UZ Engineered Prods. Co. v. Midwest Motor Supply Co., Inc.*, 770 N.E.2d 1068, 1080 (Ohio Ct. App. 2001) (stating that an "employer has a legitimate interest in limiting not only a former employee's ability to take advantage of personal relationships the employee has developed while representing the employer to the employer's established client, but also in preventing a former employee from using his former employer's customer lists or contacts to solicit new customers").

130. 54A AM. JUR. 2D MONOPOLIES AND RESTRAINT OF TRADE § 846 (2008). Other factors that courts have employed in the balancing include "the degree of inequality in bargaining power, the risk of the covenantee losing customers, the extent of respective participation by the parties in securing and retaining customers, the good faith of the covenantee, the existence of sources or general knowledge pertaining to the identity of customers, the nature and extent of the business position held by the covenantor, the covenantor's training, health, education, and family's needs, the current conditions of employment, the necessity of the covenantor changing his or her calling or residence, and the correspondence of the restraint with the need for protecting the legitimate interests of the covenantee." *Id.*

former employers, these restrictions usually must be limited to clients with whom the employee developed a relationship during the course of his employment.[131]

In the event a court determines that a covenant not to compete is broader than necessary to protect an employer's legitimate interest, the court may modify the covenant and enforce it to extent it deems reasonable.[132] Although it is true that a court will generally enforce a non-competition agreement to the extent it is reasonable, employers should be wary about reaching too far in drafting their covenants. A court may hold a non-competition agreement entirely unenforceable if redrafting would require "substantial modification."[133]

c. Adequacy of Consideration

Like other contractual provisions, a covenant not to compete is unenforceable unless supported by adequate consideration. When an employee executes the non-competition agreement simultaneously with the acceptance of employment, the acceptance of the employment satisfies the consideration requirement.[134] Even if an agreement not to compete is entered into after employment has already commenced, some courts have held that continued employment is sufficient consideration for the covenant.[135] In other jurisdictions, independent consideration will have to be offered in order for the restrictive covenant to be found enforceable.

In general, employers that utilize non-competition agreements, including sports agencies, will incorporate these restraints into the employee's initial employment agreement. Therefore, it is unlikely that inadequacy of consideration will serve as a basis for invalidating an otherwise enforceable non-competition clause.

D. In Focus: Drafting the Non–Competition Clauses in an Employment Agreement

As the discussion in the previous three sections elucidates, covenants not to compete incorporated within an agency's employment agreements are instrumental to the firm's ability to protect

---

131. *See* Michael J. Garrison & John T. Wendt, *The Evolving Law of Employee Noncompete Agreements: Recent Trends and An Alternative Policy Approach*, 45 Am. Bus. L.J. 107, 142–43 (2008) (noting emerging support for this proposition in recent case law).

132. Ferdinand S. Tinio, Annotation, *Enforceability, insofar as restrictions would be reasonable, of contract containing unreasonable restrictions on competition*, 61 A.L.R.3d 397 (1975). (This is also the law in Ohio. *See Raimonde*, 325 N.E.2d at 547).

133. Garrison & Wendt, *supra* note 28, at 143.

134. Tinio, *supra* note 29, at § 2(a).

135. *Id.* In Ohio, continued employment is sufficient consideration for a covenant not to compete. *See Lake Land Emp. Group of Akron, L.L.C. v. Columber*, 804 N.E.2d 27, 31–32 (Ohio 2004) (holding that forbearance in discharging an at-will employee serves as consideration to support a non-competition agreement).

its business. Effective drafting of these covenants is a complicated enterprise that demands attention to a variety of different bodies of law and factual issues. This section offers an overview of some of the clauses that can be included in a non-competition agreement, as well as the important considerations underlying the drafting of these provisions.

1. Background Considerations

a. The Larger Context of the Employment Agreement

In negotiating and drafting non-competition clauses, the parties should be aware of how these provisions fit within the larger employment agreement.[136] Details regarding the employment, including whether it is at-will or for a specified term, may prove decisive in whether a court will later enforce restrictive covenants within the agreement. Furthermore, an employer can enhance the legal recourse available against employees by including particular information in other parts of the employment agreement. For example, an employer can increase the prospect that a non-competition clause will be held enforceable if it incorporates a term into the employment agreement under which the employee acknowledges the necessity of the restrictions imposed in the non-competition agreement, as well as the fact that the restraints will not unduly harm the employee's ability to obtain future employment.

b. Other Legal Doctrines

Recall that other bodies of law impact the degree to which an employer can restrict an employee's post-employment activities. The importance a particular employer attaches to a non-competition agreement will be impacted by the extent to which its interests are protected under other legal doctrines. As previously discussed, although most of the agent's endeavors that an employer will want to restrain are unlikely to involve trade secrets, statutes guarding against misappropriation and the inevitable disclosure doctrine may be useful in preventing an employee from exploiting valuable proprietary information. While the agent is employed at the firm, the common law duty of loyalty will bar him from competing with his employer. Finally, an employee's freedom to pursue post-employment opportunities may also be limited by other professional obligations. For example, an agent who also operates as an attorney will be constrained by the professional rules of responsibility governing lawyers.[137] These rules may limit the contracts and business

---

136. Sample "Employment Agreement" clauses between a sports agency and its employee are provided in the Teacher's Manual.

137. Consider that when a lawyer provides non-legal services, the lawyer will be subject to the rules of professional responsibility when (1) the non-legal services are provided in circumstances which are not distinct from the provision of legal circumstances, or (2) if non-legal services are provided by an entity

relationships into which the agent may enter.[138]

c. Choice of Law

Given the fact that the law may vary widely across jurisdictions, it is highly important to be aware of which jurisdiction's law governs a contract. In particular, it should be noted that covenants not to compete are less likely to be enforced in certain states.[139] When drafting a contract, the parties should be advised to clearly indicate which state's law controls the interpretation of the document.

d. Individual Circumstances

Finally, remember that the degree to which non-competition agreements can be enforced will depend on a court's case-by-case inquiry into the particular circumstances of the employer and its employee. In negotiating and drafting clauses, the parties should remain cognizant of this fact.

2. The Scope of the Non–Competition Agreement

a. The Parties' Interests

The restrictions included within a non-competition agreement should be tailored to suit the parties' particular needs. A sports agency will differ from many other employers in terms of the interests it will seek to protect. For example, while most businesses operate on a local level and service customers in a confined geographic area, the mega-agency represents clients on the international level with interests spanning the globe. The mega-agency will be most concerned with protecting its relationships with its clients, and a provision that merely bars an agent from working within a given geographic area is unlikely to sufficiently protect the agency's client base. Therefore, as previously discussed, the mega-agency may be better served to incorporate restrictions preventing its former employees from soliciting clients that the agent represented during his employment with the agency. Furthermore, while the mega-agency cannot entirely bar its former employee from practicing his profession, the agency can draft non-competition clauses that prohibit a former employee from accepting a position with the mega-agency's major competitors. In order for these restrictions to

---

controlled by the lawyer and the lawyer fails to take reasonable steps to assure clients obtaining non-legal services that they are not receiving legal services and that the protections of the client-lawyer relationship do not exist. *See* MODEL RULES OF PROF'L CONDUCT R. 5.7(A) (2003).

138. For example, if a lawyer wants to engage in a "reciprocal referral" arrangement with a sports agency under

which each party agrees to refer clients to the other, the relationship must be: (1) non-exclusive and (2) for a definite time period disclosed to the client. *See* MODEL RULES OF PROF'L CONDUCT R. 7.2(B)(4) (2003).

139. *See Steinberg Moorad & Dunn*, 136 F.App'x at 10 (noting that the non-competition clause in Dunn's employment agreement could not be enforced under California law).

be found enforceable, they should only apply for a reasonable duration of time.[140]

b. "Reasonableness" and Reliance on Judicial Redrafting

Our earlier discussion of the "reasonableness" of covenants not to compete illustrates that these agreements will only be enforced to the extent necessary to protect an employer's legitimate interest. Given the fact that courts will tend to redraft overly-broad restrictive covenants, the agency may be tempted to author an expansive agreement in an effort to impose the greatest possible restraint on a former agent's post-employment opportunities. However, an agency should be wary of over-reaching in its restrictive covenants. As previously mentioned, in the case of some overly broad non-competition clauses, it should be noted that under certain circumstances a court may sometimes hold the non-competition agreement entirely unenforceable. In order to enhance the probability that a court will redraft, rather than invalidate a covenant that is broader than necessary, the drafter should include a clause in the employment contract stating that restraints deemed unreasonable shall be modified to conform to the law.

3. Severability

In drafting covenants not to compete, it is advisable to include a severability clause, stating that if any clause in the employment agreement is invalidated, all of the other provisions will still be enforced. This practice protects the enforceable clauses in the contract, such as covenants not to compete, from being called into question by defects in any other part of the contract, such as other restrictive covenants that may be deemed unenforceable.

The severability clause also serves to bolster the validity of non-competition clauses against an employee's argument that the restrictions should be invalidated on the basis of another challenge, such as a wrongful discharge claim. Therefore, the agreement should emphasize that each restrictive covenant is enforceable independently from the rest of the agreement and that the reasons for the employee's termination do not affect the enforceability of these provisions.

4. Non–Agent Employees

In addition to restricting the post-employment opportunities of its agents, the mega-agency may seek to limit the post-employment

---

140. Note that Ohio courts are unlikely to enforce restrictive covenants without temporal limitations. *See* Pierre H. Bergeron, *Navigating the "Deep and Unsettled Sea" of Covenant Not to Compete Litigation in Ohio: A Comprehensive Look*, 31 U. Tol. L. Rev. 373, 377–78 (2000) (noting that although Ohio courts have not issued specific guidelines regarding permissible time restrictions, covenants of one year are generally enforceable, and many courts have enforced restrictions lasting two years or more).

opportunities of other employees, such as secretaries and support staff. These employees may have acquired valuable information and possibly even ties with clients during the course of their employment. Furthermore, as agents defecting from the firm set out to compete against their former employer, they may hope to recruit other agency staff members with whom they worked during the course of their employment with the firm. Clearly, the mega-agency would like to avoid losing employees—especially those who may possess important knowledge—to a competitor.

In drafting a restrictive covenant as part of a non-agent employee's contract, the agency should recall the "reasonableness" standard these agreements must satisfy. An employer's legitimate interest in limiting the post-employment opportunities of a secretary will not be as great as this interest is in the case of an agent. Therefore, the same restraint included within an agent's employment agreement may be unreasonable and unenforceable when applied to a non-agent employee. Additionally, while it may make sense to include a restriction on soliciting particular clients in an agent's contract, this type of restraint will probably be unreasonable to impose upon a non-agent, who is unlikely to have significant client contacts.

Another method of preventing non-agent employees from joining a firm's former agent and current competitor could be to place an additional clause within the agent's non-competition agreement. For example, an agent could be restricted from being involved in the hiring of the agency's personnel, or former personnel, for a given period of time following the termination of the agent's employment.

5. Liquidated Damages

In the event of a breach of a non-competition agreement, a liquidated damages provision can have a significant impact upon an employer's ability to secure its preferred form of relief. The presence of this clause can dispense with the potentially difficult, and possibly highly speculative, inquiry into the amount the employer should be awarded as compensation for the former employee's breach. On the other hand, there are some potential disadvantages associated with the inclusion of a liquidated damages provision. A court may interpret the insertion of this clause as an admission that the employee's breach would not constitute irreparable damage to the employer's interest.[141]

Chapter 6, Part I—Negotiation and Drafting Exercise

---

141. *Id.* at 396. In general, whether enforcement of a liquidated damages provision against a former employee will preclude injunctive relief is an uncertain inquiry depending on the jurisdiction and the particular circumstances of the case. *See* 42 AM. JUR. 2D INJUNCTIONS § 125 (2008).

In light of the foregoing, consider the following hypothetical, in which an established agent and the general counsel of a mega-agency are negotiating the sale of the agent's one-man practice to the world's most prolific representative of professional athletes. Based on the readings in this chapter, advise the agent and the general counsel regarding the structuring of the agent's employment agreement, including the drafting of any non-competition clauses.

Non–Competition Clauses in Employments Agreements/ "Jerry Acguire" Hypothetical

In this hypothetical, you should assume the following facts:

Assumed Facts

Superstar football agent, Jerry AcGuire ("Jerry"), has had a great run of signing first and second round NFL draft picks to lucrative contracts with a variety of NFL teams. He has also served as the agent for the same 15–20 draft picks in negotiating lucrative off-field endorsement contracts and earned commissions at an above-market rate of 15% (the NFL agent's rate is fixed by NFL/NFLPA guidelines, whereas the endorsement contract agent commission rate is negotiable within a 5–15% range).

Jerry now wants to limit the risk of being a one-man operation and "sell" his agency into XYZ Mega–Agency—the largest player representation conglomerate in the world. At present, XYZ has a small presence in the NFL player representation area, but specializes in the individual sports like tennis and golf, and worldwide team sports like soccer and basketball. Accordingly, XYZ wants to fill out its business portfolio by adding an agency like Jerry's to its business mix. Jerry, who is also an attorney, and therefore subject to the relevant state's Code of Professional Conduct, is negotiating his own deal with XYZ's General Counsel ("GC").

In that context, Jerry's Employment Agreement needs to be negotiated in the following areas, between GC and Jerry:

1. Will Jerry's athletes become clients of XYZ after the "asset sale" of Jerry's agency to XYZ or will they remain Jerry's clients? What if Jerry chooses to let the football clients be represented by XYZ, but also chooses to remain the personal lawyer for any transferred clients?

2. What should happen to the current income stream flowing from multi-year deals with the clients' NFL teams' and off-field endorsement contracts? For example, should part of the buy-in include a graduated series of payments over a pre-determined period of time (three to five years) during which XYZ shares progressively increase from 20% to 80% to 100% of the income stream generated by Jerry's former clients?

3. What about new clients signed by Jerry, after he joins XYZ? Should XYZ retain 100% of all NFL contract and endorsement agreement commissions from day one after the merger of the two firms?

4. What about other employees whom Jerry wants to bring with him to XYZ, including his trusted Assistant, Sherry. Should Sherry have a separate Employment Agreement with XYZ? If so, should her non-comp restrictions be different from Jerry's?

5. When Jerry leaves XYZ, can Sherry go with him, or must she wait a fixed period of time before joining him? What confidential/proprietary XYZ information can Jerry and/or Sherry take with them? Is the "inevitable disclosure" doctrine applicable here under Ohio or Federal law?

6. In Jerry's non-comp, what are the maximum non-comp restrictions that XYZ can demand, while at the same time being sure that its post-employment non-comp restrictions are enforceable if/when Jerry leaves XYZ either voluntarily or involuntarily? Assume that Ohio law applies for purposes of negotiating and drafting the non-comp provisions.

   (a) Consider "reasonableness of restrictions" and a "severability clause" re: same.

7. For what "term" should the Employment Agreement be negotiated with what "outs" for each side? In particular, should Jerry retain an "out" clause if he does not achieve a certain level of income during the first one to three years of this relationship? Conversely, should XYZ reserve the right to terminate the Agreement "for cause" and/or for under-performance? What about for breaches of any common law duties of loyalty or confidentiality, if Jerry starts to plan his departure from XYZ before his Agreement term ends?

8. Should "liquidated damages" be considered by the GC in the Remedies section of the Employment Agreement, on the assumption that after a few years, both parties will probably want to go their separate ways? Consider attaching a Schedule of post-agreement income stream splits between Jerry and XYZ, based on, among other things, the length of the agreements and how personally involved Jerry was in negotiating or getting same executed.

   (a) Consider an "integration clause" at the end of the Agreement, to avoid "parole evidence" issues.

Given the foregoing facts, negotiate the terms of Jerry AcGuire's Employment Agreement, given the variables described in each of the sub-paragraphs listed in the hypothetical above.

Please use the Class Plans and "exemplars" set forth in the Teacher's Manual to help guide the class's "interactive" negotiations and drafting of this important agreement.

PART II: THE AGENT EXITING THE MEGA–AGENCY

We have now described the law governing the relationship between the agency and its employees, as well as the protective measures an agency can take to limit competition from former employees. Now, we will examine the types of claims that may emerge as a result of the agent's activities following the termination of his employment. Of course, the extent of an agency's legal recourse against a former employee will largely be dependent upon the terms of the employment agreement. As previously discussed, the inclusion of covenants not to compete and the breadth of these clauses will be critical in the agency's efforts to pursue legal action against an agent. Additionally, the agency can allege different causes of action related to the agent's misconduct during the course of the employment. This part of the chapter will address the potential claims and remedies the agency may seek against an agent who has left the agency.

A. Breach of the Non–Competition Agreement

Assume that the agent's employment agreement included various covenants not to compete. As detailed earlier in this chapter, these restraints can limit the agent's ability to solicit the agency's clients, hire away other employees from the agency, and pursue employment with another mega-agency. If a former agent were to violate any of these terms, the agency would be able to seek legal remedies.

First, the agency could attempt to obtain an injunction to prevent its former employee from continuing to compete with the firm. Injunctive relief is a powerful tool in the agency's legal arsenal. Rather than wait for clients to defect to a former agent thereby violating the terms of his non-competition agreement, the agency would be well-served to enjoin its former employee's activities before any harm is realized. Courts will enforce restrictive covenants to enjoin a former employee from competing, provided that the employer establishes that the restraint is reasonable and that the employer would suffer irreparable injury.[142] Our prior description of covenants not to compete details the factors analyzed to determine if such an agreement is "reasonable." In terms of demonstrating irreparable injury because the value of client relationships can be exceedingly difficult to calculate, courts tend to

---

142. 42 AM. JUR. 2D INJUNCTIONS § 136 (2008). This proposition is consistent with Ohio law. *See Levine v. Beckman,* 548 N.E.2d 267, 270–71 (Ohio Ct. App. 1988).

favor injunctive relief as a remedy for the breach of a non-competition agreement.[143]

Second, although lost profits may be hard to compute, the agency can sue to recover monetary damages. Damages will normally be measured according to the actual loss the employer sustains as a result of the breach, rather than the gains obtained by the breaching employee.[144] It should be noted that damages will only be awarded if material injury occurs, and consequential and punitive damages are generally unavailable.[145] For example, if an agent's attempts to solicit former clients, are ineffective damages cannot be recovered since the agency has not suffered actual harm.[146]

The drafting of the non-competition agreement will largely control the employer's ability to pursue these remedies. As previously mentioned in the first part of this chapter, remember that the inclusion of a liquidated damages provision can dispense with the difficult task of calculating the employer's loss. Furthermore, recall the effect this clause may have upon the employer's ability to secure an injunction. The liquidated damages provision may not impact the court's decision to grant an injunction. On the other hand, a court may seize upon the clause's inclusion and award damages in lieu of injunctive relief. Finally, note that the two forms of relief are not mutually exclusive, as a court can award damages and grant an injunction.[147]

B. Breach of the Duty of Loyalty

As indicated in the first part of this chapter, the duty of loyalty ceases to bind an employee after the termination of the employment relationship. However, often breaches of this duty may not come to light until after the agent has departed the agency. For example, the fact that an agent conspired with a competitor to deliver his clients to a rival agency or that the agent failed to pursue prospective clients because he planned to leave the agency may not become apparent until after the agent has exited the firm.

If the agency discovers a breach of the duty of loyalty, the firm can sue to recover monetary damages. Yet, as indicated in the first part of this chapter, courts are unlikely to grant injunctive relief for breaches of the duty of loyalty. Nevertheless, this claim represents

---

143. Richard E. Kaye, Annotation, *Cause of Action to Enforce Noncompetition Covenant in Employment Contract*, 36 CAUSES OF ACTION 2D 103, § 49 (2008). For an Ohio example, *see Basicomputer Corp.*, 973 F.2d 507 at 512 ("The loss of customer goodwill often amounts to irreparable injury because the damages flowing from such losses are difficult to compute.")

144. 54A AM. JUR. 2D MONOPOLIES AND RESTRAINT OF TRADE § 969 (2008).

145. *Id.*

146. *See id.* (noting that nominal damages may be available).

147. Kaye, *supra* note 40, at § 49.

another avenue to obtain relief against a former employee who is unfairly competing with the agency.

C. *Tortious Interference*

If a former employee has succeeded in luring clients from the agency, the firm may be able to state a claim for tortious interference with its business relationships. This claim is a tort arising under state law.[148] The elements of a claim for intentional tortious interference include: (1) a valid business relationship or expected relationship; (2) the defendant's knowledge of the relationship; (3) the defendant's intentional interference causing a breach of the relationship; (4) the absence of any justification; and (5) damages resulting from the defendant's conduct. Injunctive relief, in addition to damages, may be available if tortious interference is demonstrated.[149]

D. *Limitations*

While each of these claims may serve to protect the agency from competition with its former agents, it is important to realize that the firm will never be immune from this threat.

The agency's primary goal is to maintain its relationships with its current clients. However, even a typical non-competition agreement will not ensure that the agency's clients do not end up leaving the firm when their agent does. For example, even if an employment agreement has covenants barring the agent from soliciting former clients or joining a rival mega-agency, the clients the agent has represented on behalf of the firm will still be free to retain his services when he sets out on his own. An agent exiting the firm can simply announce his intentions and wait for his clients to follow him.[150]

Another limitation on the remedies available to the agency involves the circumstances of the agent's termination. In certain jurisdictions, if an employee is discharged without cause or if the employer exercised bad faith in the termination, a non-competition covenant may be rendered unenforceable.[151] As discussed in the first part of this chapter, however, an employer can protect non-competition agreements with language stating that the clauses are severa-

---

148.   44B AM. JUR. 2D INTERFERENCE § 48 (2008). Under Ohio law, a plaintiff must demonstrate (1) the existence of a contract, (2) the wrongdoer's knowledge of the contract, (3) the wrongdoer's intentional procurement of breach, (4) lack of justification, and (5) resulting damages. *Bishop v. Oakstone Acad.*, 477 F.Supp.2d 876, 888 (S.D. Ohio 2007).

149.   In Ohio, courts have granted injunctive relief upon a showing of tor-

tious interference. *See Brakefire, Inc. v. Overbeck*, 878 N.E.2d 84 (Ohio Com. Pl. 2007).

150.   This approach was successfully adopted by David Dunn against his colleagues. *See Steinberg Moorad & Dunn*, 2002 WL 31968234, at * 9.

151.   Kaye, *supra* note 40, at § 32.

ble and will be enforced regardless of the validity of other portions of the contract.

Furthermore, the term of the employment agreement can impact the employee's efforts to invalidate restrictive covenants. It should be noted that employees who have contracted to work for a definite term tend to have greater legal recourse than at-will employees.[152]

E. In Focus: Preparing to Litigate Alleged Violations of Non–Competition Agreements

Assume that an agent is planning to defect to a competitor of his current mega-agency employer. Further assume that this agent is bound by the terms of a "standard form" non-competition agreement, an example of which has been provided.[153] As the agent plans his departure and collaborates with representatives of a rival mega-agency, consider the following issues, which will be relevant to the hypothetical at the conclusion of this chapter.

1. Permissible "Consideration"

In an effort to convince the agent to leave his current employer for a competitor, the rival agency is likely to offer some form of payment. If the rival agency is one of the employers the non-competition agreement restricts the agent from joining, the agent may be without a reliable source of income as he waits for this covenant to expire. Can the rival agency offer to compensate the agent? If so, which forms of consideration are allowed?

Consider whether the agent's acceptance of payment from an agency he is barred from joining under the non-competition agreement may be a breach of this clause. Additionally, if the amount of the agent's compensation is contingent on his clients choosing to defect to the competitor agency, will the agent violate the prohibition on direct or indirect solicitation of the firm's clients? Finally, if an understanding regarding these payments is reached during the term of the agent's current employment with his agency, is it possible that the agent has breached the duty of loyalty?

2. The Rival Agency's Contacts With the Agent's Clients

In order to circumvent the non-competition agreement, assume that the rival agency contacts the agent's clients, attempting to persuade them to switch their representation. Is it possible that the

---

152. For example, "Ohio case law firmly establish[es] an employer's right to uphold a covenant not-to-compete after it fires an at-will employee." *Prosonic Corp. v. Stafford*, 539 F.Supp.2d 999, 1003 (S.D. Ohio Feb. 12, 2008) (citing *Lake Land Emp. Group of Akron, L.L.C. v. Columber*, 804 N.E.2d 27 (Ohio 2004)).

153. *See* "Employment Agreement," Paragraphs 6–8 in the Teacher's Manual.

competitor could be guilty of tortious interference? If the agent has discussed this approach with the rival agency, has he breached his duty of loyalty or possibly violated the non-solicitation covenant?

3. The Agent's Termination

Assume that the agency fires the agent. If the employee can successfully claim that he was unlawfully discharged, can he avoid his obligations under the non-competition agreement? Consider that the agent may have been an at-will employee.[154] Also, notice the language in each covenant stating that the clauses remain enforceable "regardless of the reason for the separation and whether it was voluntary or not." Do these facts moot the agent's efforts to void the restrictive covenants?

4. Other Agency Personnel

Further assume that the competitor agency offers to hire the agent's secretary. Is it likely that the secretary's employment agreement bars her from obtaining employment with a rival mega-agency? Would the agent's knowledge and tacit involvement in the competitor's hiring efforts potentially violate his duty not to participate in the hiring by an outside agency of any firm personnel?

Chapter 6—Litigation Hypothetical

In light of these considerations, as well as the legal background provided earlier in this chapter, please evaluate the following hypothetical.

As usual, sample forms and "exemplar" responses and Class Plans are set forth in the Teacher's Manual.

Litigation Hypothetical—Outline of "Bench Brief" re: Alleged Violations of Non–Comp/Non–Solicitation Agreements

A. *Assumed Facts*

1. Assume that Employee Number One (#1), a Team Sports Division agent, leaves Mega Agency ("Agency") and takes a number of Agency's clients with him, based on a confidential Settlement Agreement with Agency. As part of the Agreement, Employee Number One (#1) agrees to be bound by the non-comp set forth in Paragraphs 6–8 of the "form" Employment Agreement in the Teacher's Manual.

2. Assume that one year later, Employee Number Two (#2), a client executive in the Golf Division of Agency, wants to leave Agency. Number Two (#2) wants to cut the same Settlement Agreement as did Number One (#1). Number

---

154. *See* "Employment Agreement," "exemplars," in the Teacher's Manual.

Two (#2) is bound by the same non-comp set forth in the "exemplar" Paragraphs 6–8.

3. Agency says "no" to Number Two (#2) because it feels it got burned by the Settlement Agreement that it did with Number One (#1).

4. Number One (#1) and Number Two (#2) are best friends/ peers, and begin talking/negotiating re: "combining" their Team Sports and Golf Clients books of business in Number One's (#1's) new mini-Agency ("Mini").

    (a) At this time, you can assume that Number Two (#2) is still employed by Agency.

5. As described above, assume that the non-comp/non-solicitation clauses set forth in "exemplar" Paragraphs 6–8 control this negotiation.

B. *Group Drafting Assignment*

6. As a Group, begin to consider, for a "Bench Brief Outline," the following questions: What is/is not permissible "consideration" for Number One (#1) to offer to Number Two (#2)?

"The Plot Thickens"

7. In so doing, assume that Number One (#1) offers to call Number Two's (#2's) Golf Division clients, with whom Number One (#1) has never worked, and that Number One offers to service these clients' accounts until Number Two's (#2's) non-comp expires.

8. Assume that Number One (#1) offers to hire Number Two's (#2's) Executive Assistant, whom Number One (#1) supervised at Agency, many years ago.

    (a) What difference, if any, does it make to the analysis if Number Two (#2) or Executive Assistant is "discharged" by the Agency?

9. What analysis applies re: "prospective" Agency Golf Division clients, whom Number Two (#2) intentionally did not "recruit" for Agency because Number Two (#2) knew he might be leaving Agency?

    (a) Is breach of the "duty of loyalty" or "the duty of confidentiality" at issue here?

10. Assume that Number One (#1)/Mini further offers to "guarantee" Number Two (#2) an "income stream" from any of Number Two's (#2's) Golf Division Clients who choose to come to Mini.

(a) Specifically, assume that Number One (#1) offers to match the amount of money that Number Two (#2) would have made (during his "non-solicitation"/"non-comp" period) from these clients, if Number Two (#2) had been able to replicate Number One's (#1's) "deal" with Agency.

"The Jig Is Up"

11. At this point in their "conspiracy planning," Number Two (#2), while still employed by Agency, is discharged and "escorted off the premises" by Office Security after being caught, at midnight, carrying off sensitive Client information, in violation of Agency's Employee Handbook rules.

Possible Causes of Action as Agency Moves for Preliminary Injunction

12. What causes of action, if any, does Agency have against Number One (#1), Number Two (#2) or Mini, in this scenario?

    Assume further that during the pre-hearing depositions/discovery, the Court learns that before leaving Agency, Number One (#1) personally called each of his remaining Team Sports Division clients and told them that an Employee Number Three (#3), a long-time Agency executive in the Team Sports Division, would be taking over each of Number One's (#1's) accounts.

13. Consider whether Number Two (#2) and Number One (#1)/Mini are "insulated" from liability if Number One's Team Sports Division Clients thereafter expressed dissatisfaction with Number Three (#3) and chose to move their accounts to Number One (#1)/Mini, without any prodding from Number One (#1) or Number Two (#2).

    (a) In particular, what happens to the "income streams" attributable to such clients?

    (b) Please revisit Chapter 1 "post-Rep. K." income-stream "splits," to refresh your recollection re: how to "follow the money," when clients like Matty Heisman leave a mega-agency such as MESCI.

C.   *"Bench Brief"/"As Is" Group Writing Assignment*

14. "You make the call!" As a Group, work together to write the outline of a "Bench Brief". In so doing, for ease of reference, you can use Ohio law and assume a presentation to the Northern district of Ohio's Federal Court.

In the Bench Brief, recommend to the Judge what relief/remedies she should order, if any, when Agency files for a preliminary injunction to stop Number One (#1) and Number Two's (#2's) negotiations, as described above, so as to prevent any Agency clients (either Team Sports or Golf Division clients) from going to Mini.

As usual, the Teacher's Manual contains "exemplar" responses to the foregoing "hypothetical."

Index

References are to Pages

147

†